# The Second Coming of Joan of Arc and Selected Plays

## By Carolyn Gage

# The Second Coming of Joan of Arc
## and Selected Plays

By Carolyn Gage

**Praise for Carolyn Gage's plays:**

"The culture of women we have never had is invented in Carolyn Gage's brilliant and beautiful plays."—Andrea Dworkin, feminist philosopher activist, and author.

"The work of an experienced and esteemed playwright like Carolyn Gage is the air that modern theatre needs."— Jewelle Gomez, author of *The Gilda Stories,* San Francisco Arts Commissioner.

"Gage's dramatic and lesbian imagination is utterly original... daring, heartbreaking, principled, bitter, and often very funny... There is no rhetoric here: only one swift and pleasurable intake of breath after another... Women's mental health would improve, instantly, were they able to read and see these plays performed."— Phyllis Chesler, author of *Women and Madness.*

"Ever since I first saw Carolyn Gage perform her work, I have been convinced that she is one of our greatest living artists... Gage creates plays that bring the "magic" back to theatre. I have seen many of her plays performed—among them, *The Second Coming of Joan of Arc, Sappho in Love, Harriet Tubman Visits A Therapist,* and *Artemisia and Hildegard.* The impact of these performances on audiences is profound and life-changing."—Dr. Morgne Cramer, Dept. of English, University of Connecticut, Stamford.

"Carolyn Gage's writing, acting, and teaching are explosive. She rips away the cultural camouflage that permits us to accept, to be blind to, the brutal context in which women are still required to live their lives... "—Prof. George Wolf, Dept. of English, University of Nebraska, Lincoln.

"No playwright has created as amazing a pantheon of historical lesbian characters... Carolyn Gage is a national lesbian treasure."— Rosemary Keefe Curb, editor of *Amazon All Stars: 13 Lesbian Plays.*

"Rarely in my life have I left a play, or any work of art, feeling like my life was truly better for it... The plays were hilarious, harrowing, exhilarating, and affirming."—*The Spectrum*, Buffalo, NY.

"Taking in a Gage play is like getting a combined dose of Karl Marx, Betty Friedan and triple espresso. She broadcasts insight on power and powerlessness with energetic zip, laying good groundwork for directors and actors who would attempt production of them."— *WNYQ News*, Buffalo, NY.

"… strong-minded, bighearted storytelling…"—*Chicago Review*, Chicago.

### The Second Coming of Joan of Arc:

"Recalling *The Second Coming of Joan of Arc* leaves me practically speechless, but boiling over on the inside with sadness and a hunger to "right all the wrongs" of the world. Never before have I attended an event at my University that evoked tears and heartache and feelings of invincibility and empowerment simultaneously… She speaks the unspeakable truths about women's oppression that most of us are afraid to say…"—Kristina Armenakis, Women's Resource Center, University of Oregon, Eugene, OR.

"The night I saw *Second Coming* [*of Joan of Arc*], six years ago, I borrowed a copy of the play from a friend. Ever since then the book has lived in my book bag, purse, shoulder bag, carry-on… Gage has given us a hero that doesn't run around in her underwear and taught us to take back the voices in our heads. Gage has changed so many lives she will never know about. and the only way I know how to thank her is to never stop fighting."—Tamanya Marinez Garza, The University of the Sciences, Philadelphia.

"Carolyn Gage is a living manifestation of the power of articulate anger. Her play is raw, uncompromising, in your face, and her politics are no different… her passion, humour and quicksilver insight shine through her rage against the patriarchal machine."—*Women's News*, Belfast, Northern Ireland

"… unparalleled, far superior to George Bernard Shaw's… *The Second Coming of Joan of Arc* is high art and revolutionary theatre combined."—Phyllis Chesler, author of *Women and Madness* and *Mothers on Trial.*

"... passion, humor, rage, insight, regret....This play works on many levels—layers and layers and layers...a highly intelligent piece of work which always remains accessible...an emotional, moving, exciting experience..."—*From the Flames*, Nottingham, England.

"... a girl-power epic... Gage is at her best here, as almost every line is scorchingly insightful."—*The Spectrum*, Buffalo, NY

### *The Last Reading of Charlotte Cushman:*

"A tour de force... Magnificent... beautifully crafted script"—*Advertiser,* Adelaide, Australia.

"Electrifying...enormously entertaining, absorbing, and brutally honest...Anger, pride, frustration, flair, narcissism, nastiness, grandeur, passion, indomitable skill, jealousy, razor-edged revenge and ultimately heart..."—*Sunday Mail,* Adelaide, Australia.

"...unabashedly lesbian, unabashedly theatrical..."—*The Maui News*

"I almost never review something that a viewer can't see – such a show that's played only a few performances and closed. There are exceptions, however... Last week, at the Marigny Theater, I saw a one-woman show, *The Last Reading of Charlotte Cushman*, that is simply extraordinary and if there's any justice, it will return there or somewhere else... Karen Shields gives a beautifully modulated performance: moving, poignant, terribly theatrical and funny as hell...superbly structured, a showcase for a strong, dynamic actress..."—David Cuthbert, WYES-TV, (PBS affiliate), New Orleans.

### Cookin' With Typhoid Mary:

"...blood-curdling, side-splitting...out of the mouths of full-blown characters who can mount a stage and own it."—*The Lesbian Review of Books*, Altadena, CA.

### Harriet Tubman Visits A Therapist:

"...marked with originality and cleverness as well as thoughtfulness in both conception and execution....In a time in our society when slavery and its sustaining effects are never acknowledged and outright denied, it is good to read a contemporary version of the classic freedom fighter—Harriet Tubman."—Aishah Rahman, playwright and Associate Professor in Brown University's Creative Writing Program.

"... a satirical, funny and yet poignant and serious look at the abuse black women took in those days, with some interesting comparisons to today."—*The Warwick Beacon*, RI.

"vivid and evocative..."—*The Providence Phoenix*, RI

"...so powerful and raw that the audience literally could not stop cheering and clapping at the end."—*Our Weekly.Com,* Los Angeles.

"... unyielding spiritual poetry that is uplifting and lyrically profound."—*LexGo.com*, Lexington, KY.

### Artemisia and Hildegard:

"...threatened the status quo like *Thelma and Louise*...a truly remarkable play..."—*We the People*, Santa Rosa, CA.

# TABLE OF CONTENTS

# INTRODUCTION

When I was in first grade, my mother encouraged me to read a biography of Pocahontas, even though I had to ask her the meaning of every other word. This biography was one of a series written for children. I remember that the books were all bound in orange fabric, and librarians referred to them as "the little orange biographies." There were dozens of them, and I read them all.

Is that why, as an adult, I have always had such an interest in the lives of historical figures, and why so many of my plays are about real women? Certainly, it must be part of the answer.

Another part of the answer also lies in my childhood. I was raised in an environment that privileged appearances over truth, and, sadly, I learned to adapt—which is to say, I learned to perform. It was not until I was in my thirties that I began to understand who I really was and to remember a traumatic childhood history that had been masked behind the public performance of our collective social fiction.

I was blessed to awaken at a time when women authors had begun to tell the truth in unprecedented numbers, about a tremendous range of subjects: racism, classism, sexual abuse and violence against women, child abuse, incest, disability, medical misogyny. I read these writers with an excitement that I had not experienced since the days of the little orange biographies. And, just as the little orange biographies had led me out of my constricted world, these feminist biographies were leading me back into my expansive, authentic self.

As a result of my reading, I was able to reclaim a lesbian identity for myself, and, suddenly, like Dorothy in *The Wizard of Oz*, I was confronted with the "man behind the curtain," the behind-the-scenes mechanisms of heteropatriarchy. I saw how women's lives had been hidden, distorted, and appropriated. I saw how mainstream culture lied to us, and how we were complicit with these lies. The truth radicalized me, and in the face of overwhelming change and loss, I began to personify the popular feminist slogan, "Wild women don't get the blues."

*The Second Coming of Joan of Arc* was one of the first plays I wrote, and it has had an enduring popularity. After two years of attempting to find an actor willing to play the part, I reluctantly performed it myself at a talent show for lesbians. Little did I know that, twenty years later, I would still be touring the work. The play has been produced around the world in a variety of venues, the smallest being a private performance in a hospital room for a lesbian who was dying from bone cancer, and the largest being a Broadway-level production in Brazil with the film star Christiane Torloni.

*The Last Reading of Charlotte Cushman* is a play about a lesbian who succeeded in becoming the most popular actress on the English-speaking stage for four decades, using her difference to her advantage.

Later, I wrote *Calamity Jane Sends a Message to Her Daughter* and *Cookin' with Typhoid Mary,* exploring the subjective realities of masculine women and probable survivors who had been branded outlaws. These were aggressive plays about defiant women in active resistance. A decade later, *The Parmachene Belle* is a more meditative reflection on a similar theme, but with the focus on coming to terms with loss.

In *Harriet Tubman Visits a Therapist,* a woman with a dream of liberation is pitted against an assimilationist sister, who appears to have resources necessary for success. This polarity is revisted in *Artemisia and Hildegard*, a play ostensibly about the celebrated artist Artemisia Gentileschi and the mystic abbess Hildegard von Bingen. It is really about the internal split for the lesbian artist who must choose between isolation and assimilation, between starving and lying.

These plays are biographies, and they are also autobiographies, in that they reflect the issues with which I was engaged when I wrote them, amplifying my own conflicts and refracting them through the lens of a history that has been stolen or distorted.

## *The Second Coming of Joan of Arc*

*The Second Coming of Joan of Arc* was my "coming out" play. It was written in 1987, shortly after I came out as a lesbian, left my marriage, was compelled to leave my church, recovered my memories of childhood abuse, became estranged from my family, and began to identify myself as a professional playwright.

At the same time, I was involved in a high-profile lawsuit against a large state institution, in which I was a whistleblower. After turning down a settlement offer, the attorney general turned up the heat, and I found myself the target of a modern-day witchhunt.

During this ordeal, I read Vita Sackville-West's biography of Joan of Arc, and I immediately made a connection between her experiences and my own. I had already been reading Mary Daly and Sonia Johnson, and I was just starting to understand my experiences in the context of a historical oppression.

*The Second Coming of Joan of Arc* was my manifesto, and it was also my tribute to all of the women I knew who had ever been raped. It was a recruitment speech as well. I had begun to realize that my lifework lay in the field of women's theatre, and that it would not be enough to produce the work.

I was going to need to organize my own theatre, train my own actors, attract and cultivate my own audiences, publish and produce my own work, develop my own fund-raising networks, and generate radically new archetypes and paradigms in my plays. In order to do this, I would need to shut out the voices and values of the mainstream and deprogram myself from years of studying and enacting the narratives written by men, for men, about men, in theatres that had perpetuated racist, classist, gendered hierarchies. I would need to discover the lost, hidden, or appropriated works by women. I would need to track down the broken connections of my own heritage, the fragile threads connecting generations of lesbians—threads severed over and over again by homophobic heirs, literary executors, and historians. I would need to focus on intentional communities of women, however small and however remote, in order to understand my native culture.

*The Second Coming of Joan of Arc* was an attempt to recruit my audiences to my radical, lesbian-feminist perspective. The Second Coming was also an exorcism of my confused, teenaged, survivor self. I was coming to understand the sources of the anger, confusion, and identity issues I had experienced as a young woman, who was ignorant of the fact that she was both a survivor and a lesbian. So many young women go through similar confusion, and I wanted to create a character who could transform shame into pride, self-doubt into militant conviction, and self-hate into blazing anger at a system that is bent on turning women against ourselves and against each other.

### The Last Reading of Charlotte Cushman

*The Last Reading of Charlotte Cushman* is a play about the lesbian actress, Charlotte Cushman, who had been very, very famous and powerful in the nineteenth century. In my play, she is on her final tour, struggling against the cancer that will kill her.

Facing a diagnosis of permanent disability, I wanted to write about coming to terms with disease and mortality. I wanted to write about a woman who was saying good-bye to her life in the theatre.

The play was also an act of revenge against an industry that had treated lesbians and masculine woman like freaks and outcasts. Here was a fierce, fat, "bull dyke" who, notwithstanding, had been the greatest English-speaking actress on two continents in the nineteenth century! It was empowering to bring her to life, and, through her, to get in touch with my anger and contempt for the kind of colonized female roles that are the staple in mainstream theatre—roles that relegate women like myself to positions as stagehands or character actors.

The heroic performer who defies death to keep the curtain up is theatrical cliché, but I didn't mind exploiting it, because the real drama of the play lay not in the plot, but in the celebration of butch sexuality that was represented by Cushman. The real Cushman had been a major womanizer, right up to the last years of her life.

This was the Cushman I wanted to celebrate—the scoundrel, the roué. I wanted to show my audiences the special charisma of the swashbuckling butch. As Cushman says in the play, "I have always maintained that only a woman can play Romeo with any credibility." The challenge of this play was to write a fascinating, funny, tragic, charming, rollicking, rant-and-roar, tear-jerking evening of theatre based on this larger-than-life theatrical legend.

### *Calamity Jane Sends a Message to Her Daughter*

*Calamity Jane* came to me in the middle of the night. I jumped out of bed and went over to my computer, to capture the monologue as it was streaming. This was an unusual experience for me, as most of plays require months of research and dramaturgical construction before the actual dialogue is written.

I had been reading a book about Calamity, and it impressed me deeply, because Calamity appeared to have been one of the very few documented masculine women in history.

Here was a woman who was obviously some kind of gender deviant—cross-dressing and working traditional male jobs—but, at the same time, a woman who had worked as a prostitute and who was deeply invested (at least according to this book) in establishing a historical record of a sexual liaison with Wild Bill Hickok. Ostensibly, her motive was to legitimize an out-of-wedlock birth, but I thought that Calamity might well have had an ulterior motive.

Lesbian community had introduced me to so many women whose lives were absolutely heroic, and yet who were living in poverty and obscurity. Any man who had undergone similar struggles or performed similar achievements would have been a local, or even national, hero. But because of their sexual orientation, these women's stories posed a threat to the dominant culture, and their examples of strength and courage—often in resistance to patriarchy—were perceived as problematic. I was amazed and angered at the discovery of so many fierce and valiant women. I had lived thirty-four years of my life as a writer who could not find her voice, and it was suddenly clear to me that this obscuring of role models had been a large factor in my lack of inspiration.

And so I wrote a play about a proud woman who was realizing that history would deal her a bad hand. She could see that, even in her lifetime, Bill Hickok was becoming a legend of the fast-disappearing Wild West. She could also see that her life was being reduced to a joke. The male roughrider who is hard-drinking and debauched has a certain cachet that is not granted to his equally hard-drinking and debauched female counterpart. Motherhood is the only traditionally feminine role to which Calamity can lay a claim. It's her last card and she plays it with skill.

Some lesbians have questioned my valorizing a practicing alcoholic who is aggressively promoting her heterosexual credentials, but they are missing the point of *Calamity Jane Sends a Message to Her Daughter*. This play is a celebration of the survival of the masculine woman, and especially her survival in an era when there was no lesbian or transgendered movement or culture, no culture of recovery, when gender roles were rigid and proscriptive.

I am celebrating the ingenious adaptations of women like Calamity, who parlayed a traumatic or fictional pregnancy into a bid for immortality in a culture that actively despised women of her tribe. I am celebrating a woman who disguised her volcanic rage under a façade of self-deprecating humor, but whose ironic observations, nevertheless, always hit their mark.

### *Cookin' with Typhoid Mary*

Reading about the notorious typhoid carrier, I became intrigued by the fact that Mary Mallon never conceded she had a disease. In fact, she never even conceded the existence of the disease. This seeming stubbornness on her part cost her her freedom. What could be more valuable to a woman than her freedom?

I was immersed in a population that practiced habits of resistance, and I want to understand what I was encountering in my community, and in myself. The identity that is constantly under assault, such as that of a working-class Irishwoman in America at the turn-of-the-century, or that of a lesbian anywhere in 1989, must be defended by powerful strategies. The member of a marginalized minority must develop elaborate defenses, as well as generate ongoing contexts that will valorize an otherwise despised identity. When the societal pressures to erase, denigrate, and colonize that identity are pervasive, these strategies can easily cross the line into denial, paranoia, or grandiosity.

Mallon's stance as a victim and martyr cost her her physical freedom, but it enabled her to refuse an identity as a carrier of some invisible, pestilent contagion. To Mallon, a delusional, heroic self-definition—even when it meant lifetime incarceration—was preferable to acceptance of a stigmatized, imposed identity that would only allow for conditional freedom.

I wanted to write a play about the complexities of a personality shaped by the perpetual double-binds of a racist, xenophobic, classist, sexist culture. The legend of Typhoid Mary arose from the fact that the five deaths attributed to her were those of owning-class Americans, and that these people had supposedly been contaminated by a working-class Irish servant. The deaths of tens of thousands of poor folks at the hands of the rich never make headlines. The indifference of the world to the sufferings of the Irish during the Potato Famine is legendary.

### The Parmachene Belle

*The Parmachene Belle* arose from my interest in the Maine hunting guide Cornelia "Fly Rod" Crosby, whose photographs indicated a masculine appearance, and whose "spinsterhood," affinity for women, resistance to traditional female clothing, and decision to work in an exclusively male field all pointed to a lesbian identity.

I also wanted to celebrate the culture of Maine, and I took great delight in the gleaning of expressions and colloquialisms from the writings of various Maine authors. I was intrigued by the culture of fly-fishing, which seems to have achieved the status of a cult whose mysterious rites and rituals are celebrated as a path to enlightentment. I watched videos on fly-fishing, read copious books with fish stories, studied the lives of the women involved in the sport, and made a particular study of nineteenth-century treatises on the subject. One of the things I discovered was that there is a formula for the traditional "fishing story," which is repeated over and over, with minor variations.

This is the story of the fisher who is disadvantaged by age, by provincialism, or by income, who triumphs over the younger fisher, the urban fisher, the fisher with higher income and fancier equipment. Often the fisher is using a lure that has been mocked and rejected by his or her companions. The "Zen" of fly-fishing promotes the arbitrary nature of the strike as some great equalizer of humanity, a mystical, piscine agent of karma. It was a challenge to me to write the lesbian, working-class fish story.

But *The Parmachene Belle* is more than a play about fly-fishing. It is a delicate exploration of one of my favorite themes: the conundrum posed by the issue of denial. Life is so unjust, so filled with atrocity, it seems nearly impossible to function—much less achieve happiness—without denial. On the other hand, living with denial precludes engaging with life on its terms, and the one who is living with delusions could be said to be missing life altogether.

Cornelia Crosby, in my play, is a lesbian living in a time before there was even a name for what she was, much less a culture where she could find herself at home. Her tribe, apparently, did not exist. Her precarious existence on the margins of acceptable gender demarcations is endangered by a severe knee injury, for which she awaits surgery. The outcome of the surgery could end her life as a hunting guide. She shares with the audience her romantic fantasies of rescuing Annie Oakley, a contemporary of hers who also chose a non-traditional lifestyle.

Annie Oakley, a survivor of massive sexual trauma in childhood, appears to have suffered as an adult from what we now understand to be post-traumatic stress disorder. She was obsessive about shooting, and she chose to live a nomadic life, first with the Wild West show and later in a series of hotels. Her childless marriage with the dandy Frank Butler, may well have been a "passing marriage." Her strongest emotional ties seem to have been with her dogs.

Cornelia's denial is challenged when she opens Annie's gift to her: an arrow case given to Annie by Sitting Bull. In the absence of any explanatory note, Cornelia is left to interpret the meaning of the gift. She confronts the horror of Sitting Bull's murder while he was performing the Ghost Dance, his people's response to their collective genocide and extinction of their way of life. The Ghost Dance was supposed to have had the power to bring back the buffalo and "disappear" the white people.

*The Parmachene Belle* is a play about outsiders, survivors, people who have become separated from their tribe. It is a play about coming into the world with blasted prospects and hopeless odds. It is about negotiating that exceedingly fine line between denial and faith, self-delusion and affirmation, radical vision and insanity.

### *Harriet Tubman Visits A Therapist*

I wrote *Harriet Tubman Visits a Therapist* at a critical juncture in my life. It was the winter of 1994, and I had just been diagnosed with chronic fatigue syndrome. What I had been calling "a nervous breakdown" turned out to be something far more serious—and possibly a permanent condition. I needed to rethink all of my priorities and radically change my high-stress life of touring and producing controversial, radical lesbian work. The war had definitely come home, and I was not winning it.

Not surprisingly, my focus at that time was on the toll taken on radical activists, in terms of our mental and physical health, and also our relationships. Harriet Tubman was, to me, one of the most radical activists that ever lived. She not only escaped, but she went back—time and time again—to lead others to freedom. When war broke out, she was hired by the Union army and led troops against former enslavers. After the war, she devoted herself to raising the money for an old-age home for African Americans.

How did she continue to do such dangerous work for so long? Why wasn't she a nervous wreck? What enabled her to turn her body toward the South over and over, to re-enter the land of enslavement? And how did she keep going after the war, in the face of ongoing poverty and indifference toward the aged?

Of course, she was an extraordinary woman. She was exceptionally strong, exceptionally canny, exceptionally lucky, exceptionally courageous. But I am leery of the myths of superwomen. They certainly don't empower the rest of us. We throw up our hands in despair, because heroic women, we are told, are "just born that way."

Well, part of that is true, and I address that in my play. Tubman's family had remained intact for the early years of her life. Her mother had gone to great lengths to protect and nurse Harriet when she had been close to death. She learned the value of her life at her mother's knee, a rare lesson for many enslaved girls—or for any girl raised in patriarchy. The sale of her two sisters during her girlhood was a searing trauma, but one that fired her resistance instead of breaking her will. In my play, I contrast Tubman's experience of maternal bonding to the Therapist's experience with a mother who was already dissociated and broken, and who abandoned her daughter.

But Tubman had more than the strength that came from a powerful mother's unconditional love. She had an unusual spiritual faith. Reading about Tubman, I ran across this passage from a Boston paper in 1863:

> *She declares that before her escape from slavery, she used to dream of flying over fields and towns, and rivers and mountains, looking down upon them "like a bird," and reaching at last a great fence or sometimes a river, over which she would try to fly, "but it 'peared like I wouldn't hab de strength, and jes as I was sinkin' down, dere would be ladies all drest in white ober dere, and dey would put out dere arms and pull me 'cross."*

This was interesting to me, because it was not Christian. It involved "ladies all drest in white," a sacred color in African tradition. These were not women of the Bible, waiting and weeping. These were women cheering another woman on, actively reaching out and helping her to cross a line that would break the white man's laws. I felt that I had come across a partial answer to my question, "How did she do it without burning herself out?"

Tubman had a radical faith, a militant one. And it was filled with superhuman deities who looked like herself: African women. Perhaps it was ancestor worship. Her goddesses did not pray, did not counsel meekness, did not talk about a "hereafter," did not accommodate the white agenda. Tubman's spirituality did not divide her against herself. It spoke directly to her deepest needs and it sprang from her integrity as an African American woman. Furthermore, her vision assured her that, when her best efforts would not be enough, her spiritual helpers would be right there to provide what she needed: She would not be alone.

I wanted to write a play that celebrated that radical faith, but I did not want to make a judgment about whether or not her spirit guides were real. In the play, I show her vision emerging from the unbearable tension generated by her absolute need for freedom and the high probability that her attempts would end in torture, incarceration, and death. Unable to give up the dream, but also unable to commit to a path of sure failure, she breaks out of the Therapist's spell to envision a third possibility, a spiritual one. This vision is so powerful, it changes the odds in Tubman's mind. Success is now a probable outcome, one that is divinely assured. Delusional or not, it is a vision that will enable Tubman to proceed with her plan of action with a confidence that will buffer her from the ravages of self-doubt and internalized oppression. She will not burn out.

In my first drafts of the play, the Therapist was a white woman, but these efforts were too simplistic. The white therapist was clearly the "bad guy," the agent for colonization, and Tubman was the "good guy." The play insulted my audience and trivialized the issues I wanted to explore. When I changed the Therapist's identity to that of another enslaved woman, the stakes became immeasurably higher. Pitting Tubman against a woman who had achieved some degree of privilege and status in the white world complicated their relationship. It was further complicated by the fact that the Therapist had experienced firsthand her mother's disastrous bid for freedom. The trauma she had survived informed all her choices. The promise of freedom, for her, was a trap.

I wanted to honor the survivor of trauma, the woman whose mother betrayed and abandoned her. The Therapist describes accurately the odds of surviving an attempted escape. Her efforts to work within the system to offer what sanctuary and comfort she can, are not insignificant. Even her horrifying attempt to inoculate Tubman with her own traumatic memories could be seen as a kind of "shock therapy" to disabuse a patient of grandiose delusions.

The play has a happy ending, because my audience knows historically that Tubman succeeded. Secure in that knowledge, we can afford to take sides against the Therapist. For myself, applying the lessons of the play to my own life, I concluded that it was better to cultivate a system of beliefs that would endorse my activism, to live with a radical spirituality that was supportive of dreams that may well be impossible to realize, than to live a life constricted by the experiential knowledge of others. Is this inspired or delusional living?

### Artemisia and Hildegard

*Artemisia and Hildegard* was part of the trilogy of plays I wrote directly after the break-up of my radical feminist women's theatre. This break-up was a turning point for me, and, as with most significant turning points, there was a period of down time between the destruction of the old and the implementation of the new.

For me, this down time lasted from 1991 until 1997. It was a time of serious introspection, of coming to terms with the fact I had a chronic illness, of examining the ways in which I had been affected by growing up in a violent, alcoholic, and patriarchal family, and in figuring out ways to articulate my radical feminist vision in a world of theatre representing heteropatriarchal interests.

During this period of time, I wrote a book about directing and producing lesbian theatre, *Take Stage!* Ostensibly a manual, the book was also a treatise on the ways in which the traditional models for mainstream theatre do not accommodate the mores of lesbian communities. I also wrote *The Anastasia Trials in the Court of Women*, a play about the contradictions and moral ambiguities inherent in any utopian project—specifically a radical women's theatre. An interactive courtroom drama, the play leaves the final verdict in the hands of the audience. I wrote *Women on the Land*, a musical about the separatist women's land collectives of Southern Oregon, where the realities of poverty and cultural difference fell so far short of our vision of utopian sisterhood. And, finally, I wrote *Artemisia and Hildegard.*

The play was obviously inspired by the two women artists of the title, Artemisia Gentileschi and Hildegard von Bingen, whose works and lives were being discovered by a rising generation of feminist scholars. I became intrigued with the idea of a confrontation between these two giants. And, naturally, this confrontation took the form of an engagement with the most pressing issue of my professional career at that time: cultural assimilation versus separatism.

My time in Southern Oregon had allowed me to immerse myself in a separatist culture that had been in existence since the mid-1970s. I was aware that this conscientiously self-defining culture of the lesbian land collectives was unique in the history of the world, and that I was privileged to be experiencing firsthand what so many women had only dreamed of: intergenerational, self-sufficient, women-and-girl-only communities. The experiment had been euphoric and, paradoxically, dysphoric.

Hildegard von Bingen's life intrigued me, because she had begun her cloistered experience in a male-dominated monastery. Later, as her reputation attracted more and more women to the monastery, she had been able to negotiate the establishment of a separate, women-only spiritual community under her powerful leadership.

I am convinced that one of the reasons we have so much of Hildegard's work today is the fact that it was developed and archived in a separatist community—albeit one that was under the authority of a patriarchal church. On the other hand, because separatism for women can only exist in isolated and impoverished islands within a "malestream" culture, communities like Hildegard's—and mine—were and are vulnerable to defection. I was especially interested in the history of her relationship to her protégée, Richardis, because it appeared to have degenerated into a toxic mentorship—another phenomenon of closed communities.

Artemisia Gentileschi's work had always resonated with me, because of her treatment of women avenging themselves on their perpetrators. Because her themes were Biblical or classical, she was able to express an array of subversive attitudes and actions while still conforming to popular tastes in subject matter. As a radical feminist artist, I was intrigued by her commercial success with art, which was so empowering and truth-telling in terms of women's experiences of male abuse and power.

In the play, these two brilliant and exceptional women, who one might expect to be natural allies, are separated by mutually exclusive survival strategies. This antagonism reflected my own experience with other women artists, and it was important for me to locate this divergence of strategy in their personal histories, as well as in their cultural contexts. In Hildegard's case, she had been incarcerated as a child in a cell with another anchoress. She had never been allowed to define this experience as abandonment, imprisonment, deprivation, or torture. Instead, she idealized it as an act of supreme sacrifice and piety on the part of her parents—and an honor and a privilege for herself!

In my play, Artemisia, raped by her tutor and then dragged into a humiliating public trial by a father bent on compensation for his "damaged goods," chooses to deny any connection between that experience and her repeated treatment in her art of victims of rape or attempted rape. Artemisia insists on downplaying her identity as a woman, claiming that it detracts from her status as an artist—even though her paintings are militantly feminist. Hildegard, on the other hand, foregrounds her gender, even as she promotes a philosophy of art "for the greater glory of God," advocating for personal anonymity for the woman artist.

The dramatic climax of the play is Artemisia's recruitment of the audience in her attempts to break through Hildegard's wall of denial. Her efforts are not successful, and they result in deeper estrangement between the women. Although the play does not resolve the split between these women, it does attempt a compassionate exploration of their differences, and in the understanding and acceptance of these, there lies the possibility of reconciliation.

*Artemisia and Hildegard* is really a three-hander, with the projection of their art taking the place of a third character. These paintings are intended to dominate the stage with figures larger than their creators. When the dialogue between Artemisia and Hildegard enters the dangerous territory of women's violence against ourselves, the anguished figure of the rape victim Lucretia towers over them, frozen in the instant before plunging a knife into her own breast, the requisite act on the part of a Roman rape victim to "redeem" the family honor. Two separate depictions of the Biblical leader Judith and her servant, Abra, cutting off the head of an enemy appear during Artemisia's presentation, highlighting the need for alliances between women. Artemisia's failure to recruit Hildegard stands in stark contrast to this visual testimony of the efficacy of women working together against a common, patriarchal enemy.

# THE SECOND COMING OF JOAN OF ARC

**SYNOPSIS:**

Joan of Arc led an army to victory at seventeen. At eighteen, she engineered the coronation of a king. At nineteen, she went up against the Catholic church... and lost. Her trial lasted five months, and the testimony by witnesses was carefully transcribed by notaries. Twenty years after her death, a new trial was authorized, and again detailed records were kept. There was testimony by her childhood playmates, by her parents, by the women who slept with her, by the soldiers who served under her, by the priests who confessed her, by those who witnessed and administered her torture. She is the most thoroughly documented figure of the fifteenth century. So, why do the myths about the simpleminded peasant girl still pervade the history books?

Joan was anorectic. She was a teenage runaway. She had an incestuous, alcoholic father. She loved women. She died for her right to wear men's clothing. She was defiant, irreverent, more clever than her judges, unrepentant, and unfailingly true to her own visions.

In *The Second Coming of Joan of Arc*, Joan returns to share her story with contemporary women. She tells her experiences with the highest levels of church, state, and military, and unmasks the brutal misogyny behind male institutions.

One woman
90 minutes
Single set

## CAST OF CHARACTERS

JEANNE ROMÉE: A woman with a masculine
appearance, any age.

SCENE: Here.

TIME: Now

### PLAYWRIGHT'S NOTES ON STAGING

While writing the play, I kept remembering an account I had read
about a Jewish prisoner who had escaped from Poland in the early
years of World War II. He returned to his village with horrifying
tales of massacres and death camps—tales unbelievable in the scope
of their inhumanity. And he was not believed.

I envisioned this Joan of Arc, returning from the dead after the
Second Wave of feminism, to warn us of the betrayals she
experienced at the highest levels of church, state, and military.

The drama of the piece lies in the reality of her presence among us
as this survivor. It has been my experience that special lighting
effects, attempts to dress the set with tree stumps or post-modern
columns topped with manikins, "performance art" choreography,
sound effects, or multi-media "enhancements" undermine the
immediacy and urgency inherent in the circumstances surrounding
the speech. There can be no more dramatic context for the piece
than that of a complacent and complicitous audience being
confronted with their denial by an empassioned survivor bent on
recruiting them to her cause.

3

# THE SECOND COMING OF JOAN OF ARC

## ACT I

*The stage of the theatre where the play is being presented. There is a tall black stool on the stage. JEANNE enters. A woman with a masculine appearance, she studies the audience for a moment, sizing them up, like a drill sergeant at boot camp. She crosses the apron of the stage staring into the faces of individual members of the audience, making an assessment of their potential for battle. Satisfied, she squats and begins to outline the battle map on the floor.*

JEANNE: Okay. Here it is… Here's Compiègne over here. It's ours. And there's Margny, over there. It belongs to the Duke of Burgundy's men. Those are the French who are fighting for the English king—you know, the "enemy." And here's the river in the middle. And over the river is a bridge, right from Compiègne to Margny. And this bridge is unguarded. All we have to do is cross over, surprise them, and Margny's ours. Nothing to it, right?

So that's what we do… almost. We cross, we attack, they retreat. And then, suddenly, off over here… we see more of the Duke of Burgundy's men coming from the next town across the way. Well, I mean that's not good news, but it's not the end of the world either. I say to myself, "This is going to take a little longer than I thought." But my soldiers? They see these reinforcements, and you know what do they do? They lose it. Completely. They take off running back across the bridge to Compiègne, and I'm yelling at them and trying to get them to stand and fight, but there's no way to stop them. Did you ever try to stop a scared man? Yeah, right.

So I do the next best thing. I stay behind and cover their retreat. So here I am, on my horse, fighting backwards to get across the bridge, with all of my soldiers streaming past me, and suddenly I hear this terrible noise… *(Imitating a grating noise.)* I mean, it is the worst noise in the world… *(Repeating the sound.)* You know what that is? That's the sound the drawbridge at Compiègne makes when it's being raised—by my own men!

5

So, here I am, cut off, surrounded by enemy soldiers. Yeah, I'm "captured." I think the word is "ditched."

You know, when you're locked in a cell for eight months with nothing to do, you have a lot of time to ask yourself questions. Questions like, "Why the hell didn't they wait to raise that lousy drawbridge?" Don't tell me they didn't know where I was. The entire army had to run past me on the bridge to get to Compiègne. And don't tell me they thought I could take care of myself. Me, against five hundred soldiers?

Come on, what were they thinking? You know what I decided? I decided they weren't thinking at all, which in itself is a statement. They were scared. They were in a hurry. They saw me fighting on the bridge, but they didn't think about it. They did not think about what would happen to me if they raised the drawbridge. It was irrelevant.

You know, there is a term for the chapters on women in your high school history books: "nonessential information." In the brains of these men, the textbook of their personal history has two essential chapters—the one on fraternity and the one on chivalry. The chapter on fraternity tells them how to act around other men—how to be a team player, a loyal comrade, an esteemed colleague. It tells them to close ranks against outsiders and never, ever, under any circumstances to desert a brother officer in the heat of battle. The chapter on chivalry tells them that if they're on a sinking ship, they should make sure the women and children are saved first.

But you see, I was neither a brother, nor a helpless female. In the textbook of their brains, the section on me was just an insert—with a border of little cannons around it, and a heading in flowery letters, "The Maid of Orléans." It was nonessential information. They would not be held responsible for it during a test. So, with the enemy bearing down on them, they stuck to the essentials. The image of me still fighting on the bridge was entered into their programs for fraternity and chivalry, but nothing turned up—so they raised the drawbridge.

6

Now, in case you're thinking this kind of thing only happens to butch women—I say, look again. I submit that every one of you is an insert in the textbook of your country. I look out over this sea of nonessential faces, and I can see the little borders around your lives, individually and collectively. You are inserts in the lives of men. You are inserts in the history of your nation. You are inserts in the roll book of your government. And when it comes down to the real issues, we will all be missing from the program! *(Imitating the sound of the drawbridge.)*

What I am here for tonight is to take the border off "Saint Joan of Arc," and to put my life back into the main text. My story is not a sidelight of history, some piece of local color, optional reading. My story is the story of all women, and my suffering is *identical* to yours. My trial is the trial of all women. My misguided crusade is all of our misguided crusades. My enemies are your enemies. My mistakes are your mistakes. The voices I hear are your voices. And the voices you hear are my voices. *(Collecting herself.)*

In the first place, my name is not Joan. It's Jeanne. So how did "Jeanne" get to be "Joan?" It got lost in the translation. In five hundred years, a lot of things about my life got lost in the translation.

In the second place, "of Arc" makes it sound like I come from a town called "Arc." I don't. I come from Domremy. There's no such place as "Arc." It's a poor translation of my father's name—and besides that, I never used his name. I went by my mother's name, Romée.

And in the third place, I never gave anybody permission to make me a saint. Think about it. The same boys that burned me at the stake want to turn around and make me a public relations officer for their church! Right. Over my dead body.

So I'm not "Saint Joan of Arc." I'm Jeanne Romée. Big deal, right? Who cares? I care! Joan of Arc is *not* my name, and "saint" is just another word for a woman who got burned, and it's time we woke up and stopped letting other people change our names, and it's time we stopped believing it's some kind of honor to be tortured by

7

men—and most of all, it's time we started telling the truth about our own lives. These myths are killing us!

So ... Soldier, martyr, hero, saint. All between the ages of seventeen and nineteen. That is when I died. Nineteen. I just had those two years. Soldier, martyr, hero, saint... idiot.

It was my death that really did it. The beautiful young peasant girl clutching a makeshift cross, eyes lifted up to heaven, as she disappears in a cloud of fiery smoke. That was the death of "Saint Joan of Arc." Tonight I want to tell you how Jeanne Romée died.

The beginning of the end was Easter Day, 1430. I was all of eighteen. The city of Mélun had just surrendered to me, which was very exciting, because it had belonged to the Duke of Burgundy for ten years. I was standing on the walls of the city, and the soldiers and the people were all cheering me, and the bells of the church were all ringing for Easter. I couldn't have been happier. The king had been crowned; I was a national hero; everything was possible. And then I heard my voices.

My voices. Everyone always wants to know about my voices. When do I hear them? What do they sound like? Do other people hear them too? And here's my favorite—This is the one the English just would not let go of: "Why do they speak to you in French?"

My voices... My voices weren't all that special. Everybody hears voices. Everybody's got somebody leaning over their shoulder, whispering in their ear what they should do and what they shouldn't do. You know— "Get the hair out of your face! Put your knees together!" That's what civilization's all about, isn't it, listening to the voices of those who lived before you did? That's what keeps the whole machinery going. No, the real problem for civilization comes when a woman decides to invent her own voices and then believe in them. See, that's almost like thinking for yourself.

You're surprised to hear me say I invented my voices? Let's put it this way—I heard what I believed as much as I believed what I heard. I mean, think about it. Where is the reality in the voices *you* hear? Is it "out there" somewhere, or do you make them real for yourself? Just where does all this authority come from? Hey, come on, we all invent our voices. Mine were just more blatantly fictional, that's all. And that is because I did not like the selection available to young women in Domremy.

There was my father's voice... *(Imitating him.)* "Jeanne, a rich young man will come and marry you, and you will go and live with him, and he will help your poor old father take care of his sheep." And then there was my mother... *(Imitating her.)* "Jeanne, a nice young man will come and marry you, and you will go and have lots of babies, and then you will understand exactly how I feel." Oh, and let's not forget the priest... *(Imitating the priest.)* "Jeanne, God has called you to give yourself to him, and you will go and enter a convent and say prayers all day long that things will get better." All the voices in Domremy were more or less variations on these themes.

But then one day, I'm walking in my father's garden and I hear, "Jeanne! You have been chosen by God to ride at the head of the army, to take the king to be crowned, and to drive the English out of France!" Yeah... Now that's what I call a voice. It was the voice of St. Michael, and I liked it so much, a few days later I heard the voices of St. Catherine and St. Margaret.

So why saints, and why these particular saints? Well, you have to remember that Domremy was a pretty small place, and good role models were hard to come by. I mean, outside your family and your neighbors, you were pretty much looking at the sheep. If I wanted another point of reference, I was going to have to use my imagination—and I did. There was a statue of St. Margaret in our church, and there was one of St. Catherine in the church across the river, and everybody knew who St. Michael was, because he was the patron saint of the district; so, not too surprisingly, these were my role models, my "voices."

Let me tell you about them. First there was St. Michael. He led an army of angels out to do battle with Satan, and kicked him out of heaven. He was our Catholic cowboy, our superhero saint. He always wore full armor and carried a sword.

9

Then there was St. Catherine. She was arrested and put on trial for her religious beliefs. Fifty old men sat around and asked her a lot of trick questions, but she outsmarted them all, which turned out not to be so smart, because it made her sexually irresistible to the emperor who had had her arrested in the first place. And of course, when she turned him down, he had to do something to save face, so he cut off her head.

And then there was St. Margaret. Some of you are going to appreciate her. She ran away the night she was supposed to get married, and she cut her hair very, very short and passed herself off as a monk for a number of years. Now, this worked out fine, until some woman showed up accusing Margaret of getting her pregnant. Go, Margaret! But then, Margaret decided it was better to spend the rest of her life in solitary confinement than to admit she was a woman, because, as we all know, the worst—the very *worst* thing a woman can do is assume the privileges and prerogatives that men have appropriated as their exclusive domain. But they found out anyway and cut off her head.

Some role models, right? Michael, Catherine, Margaret. And guess what? I grew up to lead an army, dress like a man, and stand trial for my religious beliefs. No, my life wasn't original at all. I copied my role models just as faithfully as any one of you copy yours. Mine were just a little more flamboyant.

We have got to stop and take a look at our role models! Like maybe just spend two minutes thinking about the people we're going to spend the rest of our lives imitating? Take me, for instance. I had two female martyrs, both beheaded, and one male conquering hero. What I should have noticed was that the only happy ending was the man's. What I also should have also noticed was that a conquering male gets an entirely different reception than a conquering female. And that is because the only thing a woman is expected to defeat is herself. Anything else is not considered victory, but castration. What I'm saying is that I should have noticed I had a third act that wouldn't work. The lead part was written for a man.

What, and I mean *what*, is the happy ending for women? Marriage, where the whole company comes out on stage and joins hands

10

around the happy couple while they ring down the curtain? And they better ring it down at this point, because, as we all know, that's when the leading lady retires from the stage.

Or is the happy ending those scenes where the fatally wounded or terminally ill heroine sings her dying aria in the arms of her broken-hearted lover? The bad news is she dies, but the good news is he really did love her after all—too little, too late maybe—but, hey, who's keeping score?

Is there some happy ending for us that doesn't call for our total spiritual annihilation? What if we all dropped everything—whatever we got going right now—what if we just *stopped*, until we could figure out what that happy ending is? And not just figure it out, but see it, feel it, touch it, taste it! Because I am here to tell you, you are going to paint what you're looking at, and if we don't start coming up with something better than these female martyred saints, we're all going to end up at the stake. Today, you women are allowed to go out and work in the men's world, but when I did it back in 1430, I was a real freak. But, let me tell you, the men haven't changed, the rules haven't changed, and the institutions haven't changed. The fact that there are more of you doing it, just means they're getting ready to build a bigger fire.

But, getting back to my voices... The first time I heard them, I was thirteen. That's a good age for internalizing voices, isn't it? The age of puberty.

Puberty. I knew all about puberty even before I got there, because I had already figured out it was the missing link in the story of my mother's life.

Isabella Romée was my mother. I didn't see too much of her, even though I lived under the same tiny roof with her for seventeen years—if you know what I mean. By the time I was born, she had already had three kids and spent more than half her life married. Any time she opened her mouth, it was either wife-talk or mother-talk. The only time I ever heard Isabella speak with her own voice was when she would tell us kids about her trip to Rome.

11

See, when she was a girl, her family had gone on a pilgrimage to see the Pope, and they had taken her along. This was a big adventure—traveling all that way, going into a foreign country, staying in a different place every night, camping out, meeting all kinds of people from all kinds of places. And whenever she told us these stories, she would become very animated, and her eyes would shine, and she would literally turn into somebody else—somebody I never knew... somebody who never had children... somebody who had lived another whole life in another whole world. And this person who had had all these adventures, and who wanted to go back again, and who was brave and independent and funny—well, she was *not* my mother.

The only thing I could figure out was that something terrible, I mean *really* terrible, must have happened to turn this girl with all the big adventures into this woman who would be doing the exact same things tomorrow that she did yesterday. I didn't know what this terrible thing was, until I saw it happen to my big sister. In one year, she went from being full of crazy ideas and lots of fun, to being somebody serious and boring and busy. This terrible thing was puberty, and I made up my mind it was *never* going to happen to me.

Puberty. The beginning of periods, which means you can have babies. The beginning of breasts, which means you can nurse babies. The beginning of feeling self-conscious around boys, because you have this opening between your legs they all want to stick themselves into.

Puberty is about loss of privacy. It's about living in a body which has become public property. It's about foreign invasion, about occupied territory. One by one, my girlfriends surrendered themselves. I watched them go off with boys and turn themselves into foreigners—Mengette, Charlotte, and even my best friend Hauviette—or at least that's what I thought at the time... but that's a whole other story.

Every day I could feel my family, my relatives, my neighbors laying siege to me. They surrounded me, and they would not let anything in or out that would allow me to have a life of my own. They were

12

isolating me, trying to starve the spirit out of me—waiting for little Jeanne to raise the white flag and throw open the gates for all of them. And then they would pour into my citadel, and they would kill my soldiers, rape my women, take my children hostage, seize anything of value, destroy whatever they couldn't use, and then, when they were thoroughly in control of what little life I had left, *then* they would feed me.

I will tell you a secret. They can't threaten you with starvation, if you learn not to eat. That's right. And that's exactly what I did. I would eat as little as possible, one piece of bread a day. And it worked. My body stayed the body of a young girl. When I died at nineteen, I had still never menstruated. See, I *had* found a way to avoid puberty.

I loved myself as a young girl. I loved my body, my lean body— somewhere between men and women, somewhere where nobody could catch me. I was a freak. There's a lot of pain in being a freak, but there's a lot of respect. People have to deal with you on your own terms. They can't project their fantasies onto you. There's dignity in being a freak. I was a freak. I still am.

Let me tell you something. There's no such thing as "eating disorders" in a prison camp. There are only eating *strategies*, and mine was very successful. I did not fall into the same trap my mother and my sister did. I did not die by millimeters, as if it were my own fault. If I wasn't getting enough of what I needed to live, I was going to look like it! I was going to make the killers come out and show themselves—and they did.

But I'm getting ahead of myself. My father had a dream about me. I'm sure he had a lot of dreams about me, but this is the only one I ever heard about. In this particular fantasy, or "dream," as he called it, he saw me leaving home to go off with a group of soldiers. And in his infinite masculine wisdom and alcoholic omniscience, he took this to be an omen that I was headed for a life of prostitution. Fascinating interpretation, don't you think, for a man to have about his own daughter? It might have put his mind at ease to know that my military calling was based not on my attraction to men, but my desire to kill them.

13

In any event, this dream was a real problem for him. You might even say it had become an obsession. I mean, he tried all of the standard remedial methods of battering me and calling me a slut, but, somehow, in spite of his best efforts, I just couldn't seem to keep myself from reminding him of a prostituted woman. So, when I was seventeen, my father engaged me to a nice young man. I said I had no intention of marrying him, so the nice young man threatened to take me to court for breach of promise. I said, "Go ahead. It's my father's promise, not mine."

See, he thought he could call my bluff, but I called his. We went to court, and I won. Of course, I made a fool of my father; so after that, life at home was pure hell. And then the enemy soldiers came through Domremy and burned everything they could get their hands on.

So, you see, this was a real red-letter year for me. The year I was seventeen, my whole family turned against me and the town where I had lived all my life was burned to the ground. But these were just brush fires compared to the real catastrophe. That same year—Hauviette, my best friend—she got engaged. That did it. France's hour of glory had struck. I ran away from home.

One of the hardest parts of running away was leaving my mother. It's like in battle, when the soldier next to you gets his legs blown off by a cannon. You don't want to leave him, but there's nothing you can do for him, and if you stay behind, they'll just get you too. So you leave. Like I left my mother. But it tore my heart out.

The year before I left, she was always telling me to get married, to stop making so much trouble for my father. But way in the back of her eyes—underneath all those layers of wife and mother—I could still see those embers of her trip to Rome smoldering in her memory, like the remnants of some sacred fire at the altar of her lost girlhood. I wanted to take those embers and fan them back into flame, and then I wanted to take that flame, and live out my life—not just one or two episodes, but my *whole* life!—in the blaze of that hot, bright fire.

14

I left without telling my mother I was going, but I felt—and I still feel—that I had her blessings. I rode out with the standard of my mother's lost girlhood. I am the champion of lost girlhood dreams!

Okay. After I left home, I went to stay with my cousin. His wife was expecting a baby and she needed some help—but I didn't stay long. I talked my cousin into taking me to see the governor of the fort at Vaucouleurs. I wanted this man to give me a military escort to Chinon, where I could see the king.

The first time we went, things didn't go so well. In fact, they didn't go at all. The governor took one look at me and started laughing … *(Imitating him.)* "You better take her home before I turn my soldiers lose on her… heh, heh, heh… " Big joke, right?

So I went back with my cousin. I went back, and I thought about what had happened. And the more I thought about it, the more I kept seeing this big, red, long, hot, heavy, wool dress—the dress I had been wearing… the dress I always wore… the same kind of dress that every other woman in my village had always worn. And the more I thought about this big, red, long, hot, heavy, wool dress, the more I began to see things the same way the governor had.

You see, that dress had a voice. In fact, that dress spoke louder than I did. Before I even opened my mouth, that dress had already introduced me: "Hi. You don't know me, but I'm someone who chooses to wear this thing that is uncomfortable, impractical, and unsafe. I'm someone who chooses to wear this thing that won't let me run, fight, ride a horse, swim—that won't even let me walk outside without falling over, unless I have both hands free to hold up my skirts. Hi. You don't know me, but I'm someone who chooses to wear this thing that will make rape very, very easy for men—even though I know a lot of men will rape any chance they get, and I don't really want that to happen. So, how about it, big boy? Think you can take me seriously wearing this garment you wouldn't be caught dead in?"

Right. So I went back to see the governor in real clothes, like the kind men get to wear. And, what a surprise, this time he let me talk.

15

Now, there are a lot of myths and theories about why this macho governor gave me, a young female nobody, that escort. Some people say I must have convinced him with a supernatural prophesy. Others say he believed some legend that a woman would save France. Or that he was talked into it by other people. And here's my favorite: He was just desperate enough to try anything.

But the truth is, there is no man on earth who can stand in the way of a woman who is utterly convinced of the rightness of her actions.

So why, since we women are usually right, are we still stuck in the Dark Ages? Work with me here... Because we don't feel like we're right. Well, if we are, why don't we feel like it? Because we're waiting for permission. You will notice that my career began to slide after the king was crowned and I began to need his permission. Before that, nothing could stop me and my voices. But as soon as I started waiting for permission—I lost my timing, I lost my momentum, and, finally, I lost my confidence.

Anyway, I went to the governor, and the governor gave me the escort, and I went to the king, and the king gave me the army, and I went to Orléans, and I lifted the siege, and I won all my battles, and I took the king to Reims to be crowned, and all of these things happened for the same reason: I was one hundred per cent sure I was right.

Which brings me back to that Easter Day at Mélun, the beginning of the end. Like I told you, I was standing on the walls of the city, and the crowds were all cheering, and the bells were all ringing—and then I heard my voices. And my voices told me I would be captured soon.

My voices never lie to me. My father lied, the king lied, the generals lied, the bishops lied. But my voices, they never lie. One month after Easter, I was captured.

"I was captured." Captured, hell! Like I told you, I was *ditched*. Let's be honest. I can't even say I was betrayed. That might actually have required some forethought. No, I was ditched.

16

So, there I was, a prisoner of war. It was May 23, 1430. I was all of eighteen.

For the first few days, I actually believed I would be rescued. I believed the king would send the army to get me. I would sit in my cell and imagine I could hear their trumpets in the distance. That was June. By July, I said to myself, "Well, Jeanne, the king is holding back the troops. He is raising your ransom money."

That was July. By August, I said to myself, "Well, Jeanne, they are negotiating. Charles is having trouble getting all that money together. After all, you're not cheap." It never occurred to me that he wouldn't save me—I was the hope and promise of France. I was a national hero. In fact, I was even more popular than the king…

So that was August. By November, I knew something was wrong, but I didn't know what. The king was clearly not doing anything— but why? Like a detective, I began looking for clues among the details of my brief, but spectacular career. And I thought back a year earlier to the scene at Reims.

Okay. Here it is. It's the inside of the cathedral of Reims, Coronation Day. It's a beautiful July day, and the sun is streaming through the stained glass windows, and the bells are all chiming, and the air is sweet with the smell of incense. And the pews are all filled with soldiers, and officers, and counts, and dukes, and knights—and their ladies, all dressed in satins, and lace, and velvet.

And here are the priests, and the abbots, and the bishops. And the Archbishop of Reims is here, wearing this beautiful robe made out of gold cloth. And here's Charles, standing in the front of the church, dressed like a king, waiting to be crowned according to the ancient traditions handed down by generation after generation of French kings. And here, standing right up next to him, in the place of highest honor, is a seventeen-year old peasant girl wearing full armor… Now, can you tell me what's wrong with this picture?

See, what everyone else knew and I didn't, was that I had broken all the rules. Here I was: A peasant—Strike One! A child—Strike Two! And a female—Strike Three! Actually, any one of those is an automatic out, but I was all three at the same time. And if that wasn't bad enough, I was also illiterate, outspoken, and dressed like a man! I'm mean, we're talking about somebody so far out in left field, they're beyond the bleachers! But, all the same, there I was, right up there next to the king.

So in December of 1430, alone in my little prison cell, I began to consider for the first time the people who had been sitting in the pews that day, the people who had been so careful to follow all the rules. They passed their property and their titles down to their oldest sons, and then they passed their daughters down to somebody else's oldest son. They arranged their entire lives around their real estate—and this was considered high class!

Alone in my prison cell, I also began to consider the high-ranking officers, the ones who were supposed to be driving the English out of France—or, at least that's how I understood it. To them, the army was a career, which explains why we were still fighting the Hundred Years' War. The first rule of promotion is, "Cover your ass." This means make friends in high places, never question authority, and, above all, never, ever do anything that involves the slightest personal risk.

Alone in my prison cell, I also considered the "men of God," the clergy. They knew the good Lord helps them that help themselves, so that's what they did. They helped themselves to other people's money, to other people's land, and to other people's daughters. The name of the game here was, raise the most money in the name of the Lord, keep a low profile, and be able to cite some authority for all your actions, preferably the Bible, but anything in Latin will do.

So here is this cathedral full of people who have devoted their whole lives to playing by the rules, inching their way along, one square at a time—and along comes this peasant girl nobody, this girl nobody who has taken a shortcut right around all their precious bloodlines and titles, and who is standing right up there next to the king! This peasant girl nobody who has never held any rank at all, and she's riding at the head of the army! This peasant girl nobody who belongs to a church that thinks women are so worthless they can't be priests, and the angels are talking to her! Obviously, there is something wrong here.

I mean, here they are, these people who have spent their whole lives waiting in line to buy tickets to see God. And they've made up all these elaborate rules to make sure they get the good seats, while everyone else has to take standing room in back. And now, here's this little peasant girl nobody—walking right past the whole line of them, right into the theatre, with no ticket at all!

Now, there's two conclusions they can draw: One, they have wasted their entire lives: Their place in line is meaningless, the reservations made in their name by their ancestors are meaningless, the fact they can afford box seats is meaningless, because you don't need tickets to see God.

And then there's the second conclusion: The girl is wrong. She is dead wrong.

In December 1430, on the eve of my nineteenth birthday, alone in my little prison cell, I finally figured out why there hadn't been any rescue or ransom and why there was never going to be any rescue or ransom. I was the enemy.

So that was December. In January, the Duke of Burgundy turned me over to the church Inquisition. I was no longer a prisoner of war. I was a heretic. A woman who hears voices is a lot more dangerous than a woman with an army. Keep that in mind. *(Blackout.)*

**END OF ACT I**

## ACT II

*The setting is the same. JEANNE is seated on the stool with her back to the audience. The lights begin to come up very slowly, and as they do, she begins to speak, her back still to the audience. As she speaks, she turns to face the audience, the lights becoming gradually brighter.*

JEANNE: So… how *do* you torture a woman?

Well, you can tie her up on the rack and rip her bones apart from the sockets. That's one way. Or you can tear apart her mind and her body. Now, there's two ways to do this: You can pry her body away from her mind, or you can pry her mind away from her body. Either way, it works out to the same thing. You stop the woman. She can think but not act, or she can act but not think.

To pry her body away from her mind, you need to physically humiliate her. Of course, rape is the most traditional method, but it's not the only one, by any means. You can ridicule her body, or make fun of the things she does. You can make her self-conscious about her looks. You can make her strap her breasts in. You can make her embarrassed about her periods. You can make her frightened of puberty, frightened of sex, frightened of aging, frightened of eating. You can terrorize her with her own body, and then she will torture herself.

Now, if you want to pry her mind apart from her body, you have to make her believe she's crazy. I mean, you can haul her into a courtroom and have all the experts certify that she's mentally incompetent, but again—there are a lot of other ways to go about this. You can just annul her. We all know how that goes. Interrupt her, change the subject, ignore her, patronize her, trivialize her, dismiss her. You can deprive her of her history— oh, does she have one?—of her art—where *are* the women artists?—of her spiritual traditions—you mean there's something other than fathers and sons? You can restrict her contact with other women. You can have a *fit* over women-only space—as if the whole rest of the world wasn't "male dominant!" You can *lie* to her so chronically and so comprehensively, that the lie becomes the entire context for her existence. It's really not terribly difficult to make a woman believe she's crazy, if you control all the resources.

And if you're a real expert at torture, you can do both at the same time. You can offer to love her body, if she'll just give up her mind. Or you can offer to love her mind, and, at the same time, reject her body. That's what I got. The Church had so much love for my soul, they just had to burn my body. On the other hand, they promised to take care of my body, if I would just give up everything I knew to be true.

You think the days of the Inquisition are over? Every woman who's ashamed of her body is a victim of torture. Every woman who doubts her own judgment is a victim of torture. So just how many women do you know who *haven't* been pulled apart?

Well. My torture. As I say, I got it both ways. In the prison cell, they were after my body. In the courtroom, they were going for my mind.

I was moved to a castle in Rouen for the trial. My cell was dark and cold, and I was never allowed to leave it, except to go to the courtroom. My feet were chained to a wooden beam. It was uncomfortable, but it wasn't all that different from the other places where I had been held prisoner for the last eight months, except for one thing. I wasn't allowed to be attended by women.

In this prison, I had a special detail of guards, five of them—English soldiers. Three inside the cell with me and two outside the door, twenty-four hours a day, seven days a week, for five months. They were animals.

They insulted me, they threatened me, they ridiculed me, they degraded me. They never got tired of cruelty. They never gave me one minute of privacy. They polluted every square inch of my cell.

They did everything but rape me, but that wasn't out of any respect for me— oh, no. There were two reasons they didn't. First, I was difficult to get at, because I was wearing men's clothes. I had hose tied to the doublet at twenty points each, and I wore leggings that

21

were tightly laced. And then, my virginity was an issue at the trial—you know, virginity being equated with credibility. So after the court had me examined to certify the presence of my hymen, well, the guards didn't dare do anything after that. Not because it would have been rape. Oh no, not at all. Because it would have been tampering with the evidence.

But rape, of course, is not the issue. The fear of rape, as men have known for centuries, is just as effective as the real thing. The woman is scared to live alone, scared to go places by herself, scared of the dark, always looking over her shoulder, waking up at the least sound in the middle of the night. She is perpetually distracted, self-conscious, subverted, terrorized. She might just as well have been raped, which of course, is the whole point.

In my little cell in Rouen, surrounded by my five guards, the atmosphere of rape was suffocating. And it had nothing to do with sex. It had to do with degradation. They wanted to make me despise myself. I chose to despise them instead.

Anger is a discipline. I practice my anger the way some people practice piano. It takes energy to be outraged. It's hard work. Especially when the abuse becomes routine. Some days I was tired and sore and feeling sorry for myself. Some days I just wanted to pretend I didn't hear them. Some days I wanted to pretend I was above it all. But I would always say to myself, "Jeanne, if you don't resist this abuse, then you accept it, and if you accept it, then you deserve it, and if you deserve it, you are a dead woman—and that's exactly what they want!"

So no matter how sick, how tired, how weak I was, I would always rise to the occasion, throw back the insult, protest the abuse, and demand my rights as a human being. Of course, this had no effect on them, but it kept me alive.

I want to say something about my experience. I hear a lot of talk about women forgiving men. I don't believe in it. I have experienced almost every form of cruelty men can inflict on women, and I am here to tell you that no woman can forgive it or ignore it, and furthermore no woman should ever try. There is no such thing

22

as forgiveness. There is only resolution. With abuse, you either resist it or you accept it, period. Anything else is just fooling yourself.

So I fought for my body in the cell. In the courtroom, I had to fight for my mind.

Let me tell you about my trial. I had two judges, two officers of the court, three notaries... and an usher to escort me back and forth from my cell... and thirty-two doctors of theology, sixteen bachelors of theology, four doctors of civil rights, seven men with special licenses, five doctors of canon law, fifteen men with licenses in canon law, seven medical doctors, eleven masters of arts, sixteen assistants and expert witnesses, twenty-three priests, five bishops, three abbots—and a cardinal, in a pear tree. After all, you can't be too careful with these teenage girls.

The trial lasted five months. It focused on two issues—my voices and my clothing. Now, that seemed strange to me at first, because both of those things are so irrelevant. I mean, why would all these important men be so interested in things that were so personal? I kept trying to skip over their questions or change the subject, but time after time, day after day, they kept coming back to those same two things: my voices and my clothes. Of course. My perceptions and my identity. They knew exactly what they were doing. They wanted me to renounce my voices—that is, to invalidate my perceptions, and to wear a dress—that is, to alter my identity to suit them. Of course. Haven't we all?

And there was something else they were very interested in. My attempt to escape. Men are always fascinated by women's attempts to escape, but only if we fail. If we succeed, they pretend we don't exist—which answers the question about what happened to all the women artists. My attempted escape? I had jumped off the roof of the castle where I had first been held prisoner. This was very interesting to them, because they thought I might have been trying to kill myself. I don't know how they came up with that. The tower was only seven stories high.

23

The reason they were so fascinated with this little episode was because trying to kill yourself is considered a sin. What I want to know is why isn't it a sin to *make* a woman want to kill herself? Probably because that would put the Pope on the Ten-Most-Wanted List. So they kept asking me over and over, "When you jumped, weren't you trying to kill yourself...?" "When you jumped, weren't you trying to kill yourself...?" And I would always answer, "I was trying to escape." Like there's some difference.

So they didn't get what they wanted, but it didn't matter, because the fact I didn't die from a seventy-foot drop, proved I was a witch anyway. And, you know—there, I have to agree with them. Most of us women who survive our own best efforts at self-destruction are pretty miraculous, don't you think?

So on and on it went. Actually for a while, I was holding my own. They'd ask these idiotic questions, as only men in positions of authority can do, like... *(Imitating the men.)* "Jeanne, do St. Catherine and St. Margaret have hair?" Watch out! Trick question! So, I'd say, "Well, I can certainly see why that would be important to know." Or... *(Imitating again, one hand suggestively in her pocket.)* "Now, Jeanne... hmm... when St. Michael appeared to you, was he... hmm... wearing any clothes?" And I'd say, "What do you think? God's too poor to give him any?" A lot of people in the courtroom would crack up. In fact, I think a lot of them were secretly rooting for me.

I think my judge Cauchon knew it too. I was supposed to have two judges, but one of them never showed up. Really, it was Cauchon's baby. He told everybody he wanted to have a "beautiful trial." It was going to be a big boost for him. You see, he was on a career track. He had gone to the University of Paris, and then they sent him to Rome, and then they made him the Bishop of Beauvais, so he was moving right up the old ladder.

But then he ran into a snag with the war, and he had to choose which side to be on. Since all his rich friends in Beauvais were for the English, he decided he was too, which worked out fine until I came along and the French started to win. Two years before this trial, all his hot-shot friends got kicked out of Beauvais, and he lost

24

his territory. So now this refugee bishop was going to use this trial to stage his big come-back. That's why he invited all these prominent people to see it. And here I was, making a monkey out of him!

Let me tell you something about men... They can't stand to lose face. It's difficult for us women to understand how very, very important this is to men, because we have never been allowed to have enough face to lose. Women tend to be more concerned with things like the justice of an issue, or finding a peaceful solution. It's difficult for us to understand how the most important thing, even in the case of war, is to find some way for all of the men involved to save face. It would almost be funny how childish they are, except that these "children" are running the world—and they have almost ruined it.

And these rules of face-saving are hard on women. When a woman challenges a man, it's not enough for him to prove she's wrong. In order to save face, he has to annihilate her. And this is what Cauchon was out to do.

After my sixth day in court, he moved the trial to my little cell. No more audience. Just him, a few assistants, and the notaries. Things went downhill for me. Without the pressure of the spectators, I couldn't make him skip over the questions any more. I had to give him what he wanted.

And when it was all over, five months and hundreds of pages later, this is what they came up with. Here are my charges: One, disobeying my parents and causing them anxiety. I kid you not. Two, wearing men's clothes. Three, taking a vow never to have sex with men—can't imagine why. Four, listening to voices on the sole basis they brought me comfort. Five, believing in these voices without the church's permission. Six, refusing to recognize the church's right to judge my actions.

These were my crimes. And if you think they don't burn women for these anymore—ask any dyke. She'll tell you.

So they take me out of my cell. They take me to a cemetery—that's appropriate, isn't it? And there are these two big platforms they've built just for the occasion. This one here for me, and that one for the judges. And over there is the little cart with the executioner, waiting to take me to the public square, where the stake is.

And I want you to imagine for a minute, all around you, all over this room, a sea of faces—ignorant, vicious faces. Faces of people who have come to watch you die. Faces expecting your death—no, insisting on it! Faces that should be familiar: working class faces, faces from your own neighborhood, faces of old women like your grandmother, faces of little girls like your sisters— human faces. And all of them are completely unrecognizable.

There is not one glimmer of sympathy, not one spark of compassion. They are all looking at you, but they don't see you. They see their long-awaited revenge; they see their promised entertainment; they see their reward for living cowardly and conservative lives. The world owes them your death—and they're going to get it!

I had been in battle before. I had expected to die many times. Yes, I had even tried to kill myself. But nothing in my experience had prepared me for this—for these hideous faces. Fear is one thing, but this… this was horror.

So while they were reading my sentence, I broke down and confessed. I renounced my voices and promised to wear a dress. What happens to women when we finally do break—which is usually after almost superhuman suffering? Do we win a reprieve? Are we released, forgiven? Does the torture stop, the pressure let up? I have seen all kinds of women give in in all kinds of ways: to harassment, to guilt, to sex, to drugs, to alcohol, to mental illness. And in every single instance—listen to me!—the abuse increases. There is no mercy for women, because our crime is our sex. We have got to fight.

So, I confessed. And, like most women, I expected some reward for surrendering myself, for betraying my voices, for denying my purpose, for selling out every single scrap of my integrity. I expected I would be moved to a church prison where there would be other women prisoners and women attendants. But that didn't happen. They took me back to my old cell, back to my five guards. Only now I was wearing a dress.

Meanwhile, the crowd with the faces was starting to get ugly. They didn't care anything about heretics, or laws, or procedures, or confessions. All they wanted was to see somebody suffering more than they were. When they realized they had been cheated out of an execution, they were ready to riot. So, you see, the political pressure was building to find some way to make me break the terms of my penance.

It was on Thursday when I signed the confession and they took me back to my cell. On Saturday, the guards opened the door and let an Englishman into my cell. He was well-dressed, and I thought he must be a lord or something. I stood up and faced him to see what he wanted. He said my name, "Jeanne?" "Yes?" Wham! "The Maiden?" Wham! And I'm on the floor, and he kicks me in the ribs, in the stomach, and I roll into a ball. He's kicking my back and my legs. And then he's on the floor over me, and he's pulling up my dress—with one hand!

If I had been wearing men's clothes, he would have had to use both hands. He would have had to untie forty knots and two sets of lacings—with both hands! I would have made him pay for it, you better believe it. But with a dress? One hand, one movement. That's what dresses are about, isn't it? Accessibility? I don't see where that's changed much in five hundred years. And neither has rape.

So he's got my skirt up, and I'm lying on the floor, and he's smacking my face back and forth. Wham! Wham! Wham! And with his other hand... with his other hand, he's taking out his... penis. And here's my precious girl body—my own sweet body—my body, me! It's me! And he's jamming this big ugly thing into my sweet body! And he's slamming into my body. Wham! Wham! And I can't focus my eyes, and my nose is bleeding, and he's talking between his teeth in some language I can't understand. And then suddenly he's standing up and kicking me again. In the uterus, in

reach me to do his job. I had a little wooden cross inside my clothes, against my chest. A priest sent to a church in the square for the ceremonial cross, and he held it up so that I could see it. And they tied me to the stake and lit the fire.

Between the time they lit the fire and the time I lost consciousness—was a long time. It was a long time to wonder where God was. The God I had been taught to believe in was no match for my suffering. My voices were still with me. They're always with me, because they're part of me, but where was this loving Father with all the power to save people, or at least to make me die quickly?

Do you remember when Dorothy exposed the Wizard of Oz, and you heard the booming voice say, "Pay no attention to the man behind the curtain"? Well, let me tell you, when we women begin to expose the actions of men, we hear this sacred voice urging us to protect and forgive. This voice is so ancient, so powerful, so authoritative that we're overcome with guilt and shame—even though *we're* the victims!

I'm here today to tell you something about that voice. That voice telling you to protect and forgive men, that voice urging you to be a little more patient, a little more tolerant—that is not the voice of God. It's the voice of the men behind the curtain. The only reason it sounds like God is because they have been amplifying themselves for two thousand years and using a lot of special effects.

Tied to that stake, watching the fire come closer and closer, I realized that God the Father was a lie. He's an invention of the good old boys to cover their tracks and their asses. I realized that the closest I had ever come to any real sense of spirituality was alone with my voices, or in the company of other women.

I realized what a fool I had been to waste my time crowning some man king, as if he had some divine right to rule. I realized what a fool I had been for trusting a church run by men who only worshiped themselves and each other. I realized what a fool I had been to lead one army of men out against another, as if it could make any possible difference which side won. And I realized what a fool I had been to believe I would be saved from the actions of men by a god they had created in their own image.

God the Father was a lie then and is a lie now, and all the hierarchies modeled after him—the governments, the armies, the churches, the corporations, *the families*!—are illegitimate. We will not reform them. They will martyr us. *We will never reform them.* We must fight for our own causes, women's causes. We must clothe ourselves in self-respect, arm ourselves with our finely-tempered rage, and obey only those voices that we women alone can hear. *(An awkward pause, as JEANNE realizes that she has one more betrayal to expose.)*

So. "Saint Joan of Arc". Twenty years later they had a second trial to "rehabilitate" me. You see, I was holding my own as a national hero, and if there's one thing the Church can't stand, it's competition. Besides, the myth of a feminine, simple-minded peasant girl had begun to replace the memory of the cross-dressing butch with the smart mouth.

Well, this second trial was pretty much a formality without the star witness. Everybody knew ahead of time what the outcome would be. Not much interesting, except for one thing. Hauviette—my best friend—she testified. I didn't think she'd even remember me.

I remembered her. Hauviette and I had been very, very close, until the year I ran away. We had grown up together. We had taken our first communion together, which was a very special thing. See, it was a custom in my village for the girls who shared their first communion to sleep with each other. She would come over to my house, or I would go over to hers. We would sleep in the same bed together.

And sometimes we would pretend we were on a very small boat in the ocean, and I had rescued her. I would hold her in my arms, and my heart would be so full of tenderness, it would make me feel light-headed. Or sometimes we would pretend that she had found me wounded in the forest and had taken me to her cottage, where she would bandage my wounds and cover me with kisses. *(Remembering.)* We were girls... Hauviette and I were more than

31

best friends. We were one soul. We knew this, and we had always planned to live together after we grew up. But, like I said, there was this terrible thing, puberty.

Hauviette got engaged. I wouldn't even speak to her. How could she do that to me, after I had gone to so much trouble to break off my engagement? So I left Domremy. I left, and I didn't tell her I was going. I said good-bye to all my other friends—but not to her.

Anyway, here she is twenty years later, testifying. And what does she say? She says she cried her eyes out when she heard I had left Domremy. She says she loved me because I was so good. And then she described how we used to lie in each other's arms like lovers. That's what she said. You can look it up. It's in the transcripts. She's forty years old and married, standing in front of a room full of Catholic priests and judges, and she says this about a girl who's been dead for twenty years, a girl who left her without saying good-bye.

Hauviette. She had more courage than I did. It was easier for me to face the English army, the French Inquisition, and even the executioner than to look at her and say, "I love you." There is one crime I committed. It's one they overlooked in my trial, but it's the one for which I suffered the most—the one for which I suffer every day. I confess it. I denied my love for a woman, and I denied the woman who loved me.

So there was no "Saint Joan of Arc," with her legacy of glorious martyrdom. But there was a Jeanne Romée who made the terrible, terrible mistake of trying to find a substitute in the world of men for the love she had experienced in the arms of a woman. *(She begins to say something else, changes her mind, and exits abruptly.)*

### BLACKOUT

### END OF PLAY

# THE LAST READING OF CHARLOTTE CUSHMAN

**Synopsis:**

*The Last Reading of Charlotte Cushman* is a one-woman show about the greatest American actress of the nineteenth century. Charlotte Cushman, a large woman of masculine appearance, was very "out" about her lesbianism, cross-dressing to play men's roles and referring to her partner as "my wife."

The play opens with an announcement that the performance will be canceled, but Charlotte, outraged that such a decision has been made without consulting her, charges on to countermand the order. Cushman, struggling desperately against breast cancer, insists on performing—and, taking up the challenge of her condition, devotes the evening to the subject of death. Having played many roles which require dying, Charlotte regales the audience with moving—and sometimes hilarious—scenes from *Macbeth, Hamlet, Oliver Twist, A Midsummer Night's Dream, Henry VIII*, and the notoriously bad melodrama, *Guy Mannering.*

Interspersed with her monologues are anecdotes about other actors, her family, and about the romantic intrigues of the lesbian community of American émigrées who were living in Rome in the mid-1800's. This community included Harriet Hosmer and Emma Stebbins, both sculptors of international reputation.

One woman (plus one very brief, walk-on part)
90 minutes
Single set

## CAST OF CHARACTERS

STAGE MANAGER:  A man or woman of any age.

CHARLOTTE CUSHMAN:  A large woman, masculine
      in appearance, late 50's.

**SCENE:** The scene for the reading is the actual theatre where the play is being produced.

**TIME:** The present.

# THE LAST READING OF CHARLOTTE CUSHMAN

## ACT I

*Lighting is set at pre-show levels. An antique table and chair are center stage. On the table is a pitcher of water with a glass, and next to them is a stack of old books with markers in them. An elegant vase with an arrangement of flowers graces the table. The STAGE MANAGER enters, uncomfortable to be addressing an audience.*

STAGE MANAGER: Could I have your attention please? I've been asked to announce that the reading tonight has been cancelled. It seems that the performer is ill, and she won't be able to appear—

CHARLOTTE: *(From the wings.)* Just a minute! Just a minute! *(CHARLOTTE CUSHMAN enters. She is a tall, white-haired woman in her late fifties. She is masculine in appearance and comportment, and she wears her hair pulled back off her forehead. Her outfit is unorthodox, but it suits her well. She wears a man's tailored jacket and tie from the 1870's over a long, full skirt of dark color. CHARLOTTE is a proud woman, fiercely in control of her own destiny. Her life has been the theatre, and her relationship with her public has always taken precedence over her relationships with lovers or friends. She is dying, and she knows it. This will be her last stand, and she pulls all the stops. She enters, out of breath.)* What do you think you're doing?

STAGE MANAGER: *(Turning in surprise.)* Miss Cushman—

CHARLOTTE: Who told you to cancel my reading?

STAGE MANAGER: They said you had collapsed in the dressing room.

CHARLOTTE: *(Enraged.)* Yes, and I have expanded again. I want to know whose idea it was to cancel the reading.

STAGE MANAGER: It was Miss Stebbins, your... your...

CHARLOTTE: *(A challenge.)* My wife? *(Enraged, she turns toward the wings to confront Emma.)* Yes, well, Emma tends to overreact sometimes. *(To Emma.)* Don't you? *(To STAGE MANAGER.)* I'm sure Emma told you all about my cancer, didn't she? My *breast* cancer? *(To Emma.)* Yes. *(To STAGE MANAGER.)* And did Miss Stebbins tell you that it was my cancer that brought me out of retirement four years ago? And did Miss Stebbins tell you that in these four years of touring, I have performed hundreds of readings and plays? *(To Emma.)* No? *(To STAGE MANAGER.)* And did Miss Stebbins tell you that in all these years, I have never missed a single performance? *Never?* *(To Emma.)* No? *(To STAGE MANAGER.)* But, if you and Emma feel that it would be better for me not to go on, I will be happy to withdraw… *(Scooping up her books.)* … *after* I have collected my full fee, of course.

STAGE MANAGER: *(An agonizing pause, during which the STAGE MANAGER turns first to Emma and then back to CHARLOTTE.)* Miss Cushman, if you're willing to—

CHARLOTTE: *(Dropping the books.)* Thank you, I am. Now, if you'll just introduce me, I think we can get on with our evening. *(She hands her/him a card and turns her back.)*

STAGE MANAGER: *(Glancing in Emma's direction before reading the card.)* "Ladies and gentlemen, it is my privilege tonight to present the greatest English-speaking actress of two continents, a performer who has entertained for three presidents and the crowned heads of Europe, an American artist whose interpretations of Shakespeare's tragic heroines are legendary, and a leading lady for four decades…" *(With a flourish.)* … Ladies and gentlemen—Miss Charlotte Cushman! *(The STAGE MANAGER exits, and the lights come up on the set. CHARLOTTE turns to acknowledge the applause. She is still stung by Emma's interference.)*

CHARLOTTE: Well… *(Picking up the books.)* I was preparing to read a little Tennyson for you… and a little Bobby Burns… and some of Mrs. Browning's poetry tonight, but since Miss Stebbins has taken it upon herself to select a theme for this evening—death— I am afraid that the readings I had prepared are no longer suited to the occasion. Well… *(Pushing the books to one side.)* I shall just

38

have to improvise. Death... *(She crosses to the table and takes a drink of water.)* The first time I encountered death, I was twenty-three years old and in bed with a prostitute. *(Sitting, she turns to the audience.)* That got your attention, didn't it? *(Turning toward Emma in the wings.)* See what you've started? *(To audience.)* This is all Emma's fault. *(A long look at Emma before she turns back to the audience.)* So—where was I? Ah. In bed with a prostitute.

Well, I was twenty-three years old and living in New York. I was what they called a "walking lady," which is the actor who takes the roles too large for the chorus and too small for the leads. This was at the Park Theatre. And it was excellent training, too. Everything was repertory in those days, and during my three years as a "walking lady," I performed over a hundred and twenty different roles. But what does this have to do with a prostitute?

I'm getting to it. The Park Theatre was managed by one Stephen Price, and it is an understatement to say that Mr. Price and I did not get along. You see, Mr. Price resented any actor who was more handsome than himself. *(She laughs.)* He saw it as his personal mission in life to drive me out of the company, and in February of 1839, it looked as if he just might succeed.

The Park Theatre was going to produce *Oliver Twist*, and there is a part of a prostitute in the play, Nancy Sikes. Well, in my day, no actress with any kind of reputation would touch a role like that, and Stephen Price knew it. So, naturally, he assigned it to me. If I took the part, I would be professionally ruined, and if I refused, I would be fired. Yes, Mr. Price finally had me where he wanted me.

And to tell you the truth, I considered quitting. It was quite an insult to be cast as a prostitute, and of course, he had done it in front of the whole company. But I had seen too many talented women lose out to temperament in this game, and I was determined not to be outmaneuvered. If there was a way to play Nancy Sikes without damaging my reputation, I was going to find it. And I was equally determined to see Stephen Price hoist on his own... *(Pausing to consider.)*... tiny petard. *(Laughing, she rises.)* So I accepted the part—graciously. And then I took myself down to Five Points. That was the area just east of Broadway—the worst slum in New York.

39

And I rented myself a room at Mother Hennessey's, which was the cheapest and dirtiest rooming house I could find. That was where the streetwalkers and the drunks stayed, when they could afford a roof for the night. And it was there, at Mother Hennessey's, that I began to study the role of Nancy Sikes.

During the day, I went out on the street and watched the old women pick through the garbage, and then I watched the young women pick through the old men. I watched their hands, their hips, their elbows, their mouths, their teeth, their eyebrows. I watched them flirt, I watched them joke, I watched them steal—I watched the things that no one else was watching. And at night, I went to the saloons, and I studied the women there. *(Smiling.)* And sometimes the women studied me. On the third night, a young prostitute came into the bar. She was very sick, shaking all over, and she asked for water. They gave her a glass of whiskey, and she got sick all over the floor. The men thought this was funny. *(A long pause.)*

I went to help her, and it turned out she didn't have any place to stay for the night, so I took her up to my room at Mother Hennessey's, I undressed her, I helped her to bed... *(Pausing.)* And then she died. *(She sits.)*

That's it. That's the story. No last words, no touching prayers, no anxious faces hovering over the bed, no final embrace. A convulsion and she died. That was it. *(Reflecting.)*

> *"... Out, out, brief candle!*
> *Life's but a walking shadow, a poor player,*
> *That struts and frets his hour upon the stage,*
> *And then is heard no more. It is a tale*
> *Told by an idiot, full of sound and fury,*
> *Signifying nothing."*

What did I do? I took her clothes. *(Rising with mock indifference.)* Of course, I took her clothes. I had a show to open, and they fit me... *(With anger.)* And then I went back to the Park Theatre, and I gave them Nancy Sikes. Oh, yes, I gave them Nancy Sikes. Not the whore with the heart of gold, not the feisty little spitfire from the wrong side of town—oh, no—I gave them a prostitute the likes of which they had never seen on a New York stage, even though they passed a dozen girls just like her on the way to the theatre—even though half the men would go home with one of these girls on their arm.

But I gave them a prostitute they could see, not just look at—but really see. I gave them a prostitute that made them weep the tears that no one shed that night at Mother Hennessey's. And weep they did. You see, real life is too painful for most people. That's why they come to the theatre.

So—would you like to see Nancy? You would? All right. This is from the third act, where the boy Oliver has been kidnapped by Nancy's pimp, Fagin. Her boyfriend, Bill, is threatening to turn his dog loose on Oliver, and Nancy is determined to stop him. Here's Bill... *(Turning away to get in character as Bill Sikes.)* "I'll teach the boy a lesson. The dog's outside the door—"

*(As Nancy.)* "Bill, no! He'll tear the boy to pieces."

*(As Bill.)* "Stand off from me or I'll split your skull against the wall!"

*(As Nancy.)* "I don't care for that, Bill. The child shan't be hurt by the dog unless you first kill me."

*(As Bill.)* "Shan't he? I'll soon do that if you don't keep off."

And here comes Fagin: *(As Fagin )* "What's the matter here?"

*(As Bill.)* "The girl's gone mad."

*(As Nancy.)* "No, she hasn't."

*(As Bill.)* "Then keep quiet."

*(As Nancy.)* "No, I won't... Now, strike the boy, if you dare—any of you! Don't "dear" me! I won't stand by and see it done! You have got the boy, and what more would you have? Let him be then, or I will put that mark on you that will bring me to the gallows

41

before my time! Oh, yes, I know who I am and what I am. I know all about it—well—well! God help me! And I wish I had been struck dead in the streets before I had lent a hand in bringing him to where he is. Ah, me! He's a thief from this night forth—and isn't that enough without any more cruelty? Civil words, Fagin? Do you deserve them from me? Who taught me to pilfer and to steal, when I was a child not half so old as this?—You! I have been in the trade and in your service twelve years since, and you know it well—you know you do! And, yes, it is my living! and the cold, wet, dirty streets are my home! and you are the wretch who drove me to 'em long ago, and that'll keep me there until I die—" *(She lunges, as if to strike Fagin.)* Devil!"

*(The gesture tears open CHARLOTTE's mastectomy scars, and she freezes in pain, her hand covering the place. Glancing toward the wings, CHARLOTTE holds up her hand to prevent Emma coming onto the stage.)*

No! I'm all right, Emma. I'll be fine – *(Turning her attention toward the table.)* I just need a little water... and I'll be fine. *(Sitting, she concentrates on pouring the water. She gestures toward the wings, in order to divert attention from her condition.)* Emma. Emma Stebbins, my wife. *(CHARLOTTE forces a laugh.)* Emma and I have been together—what?—twenty years now? *(She looks toward the wings, in need of Emma's support.)* Nineteen? *(Relieved at Emma's response, she turns to the audience.)* Nineteen years. Emma's counting. Emma Stebbins, the world-renowned sculptor. We met in Rome. Emma was living with Harriet Hosmer – *(She turns toward the wings. Emma has apparently said something.)* What? Oh, it's all right. They don't care. *(To audience.)* Do you? I didn't think so. *(To Emma.)* See? They don't care. *(To audience.)* Emma was living with Harriet Hosmer. She is a sculptor, too. An excellent sculptor. Harriet Hosmer—Hatty. *(To Emma.)* May I tell them about Hatty? I know they want to hear about her. Everybody wants to hear about Hatty. May I? *(Emma has said something.)* What? *(Defensive.)* What about Rosalie? *(Pause.)* All right, I will... *after* I tell them about you and Hatty. *(To audience.)* Emma's a little touchy about Hatty.

Well—Hatty Hosmer. Hatty's not speaking to me now. Something about our hunt club in Rome. Hatty didn't think it was fair that they never gave the tail—the fox tail—to the Americans. Of course, she's talking about herself. Hatty's always talking about herself. But I have to admit, she can ride the pantaloons off the Italians. But there was no need to blow the whole thing into an international incident, which is what she did. Well, apparently she felt I didn't give enough support to her cause. So now she's not speaking.

But it's not really about fox tails. It's about death. I know Hatty. She lost practically her whole family before she was twelve. Her mother died when Hatty was six, and then she lost her two brothers, and then her sister. I just don't think she can take anyone else dying on her. So, you see, she's decided to kill the friendship instead.

But you want to hear the scandal. Well, I met Hatty Hosmer in 1851. I was thirty-five, and she—bless her heart—was just twenty-one. And a cuter little tomboy you never saw. Oh, she was a wild thing! Reminded me of myself. Anyway, I was touring in Boston, and she had just come back from medical school. She had been taking anatomy courses for her sculpting. Of course, she was the only woman they let in the school. That was Hatty. *(Rising.)* Well, she came backstage to see me, and, frankly, she was quite smitten. And, to tell the truth, I was rather dashing in those days—prancing around in tunics and tights... I had good legs. Still do. *(She shows us.)* Anyway, Hatty started coming backstage after every performance—and bringing me flowers. *(She shakes her head at the memory.)* It was very sweet.

But I was married at the time—to Matilda Hays, and Matilda did not think it was so sweet. Matilda and I were having some problems. Oh, Matilda... *(She sits.)*

She had shown up at my door in London—not unlike the way Hatty was showing up in Boston—asking me for acting lessons. It has always amazed me how many young women seem to be in need of my instruction.

Well, as luck would have it, I had just lost my touring partner, and I was in the market for a new Juliet for my Romeo. How's that for a line? *(Laughing.)* Worked, too. Matilda auditioned for me, and I cast her, and we became lovers on and off the stage. It was all very daring and very romantic, and we were so pleased with ourselves, we got married. That's right. We had a ceremony and exchanged vows of celibacy—referring to men, of course—and promised to be faithful for eternity. *(Laughing.)* And it *was* an eternity. *(Another burst of laughter.)*

It turned out that Matilda was not really up to the demands of a touring performer, and she retired from her public role as Juliet, but she continued to accompany me as my wife. She told me she was happy, and I believed her. I have never understood a woman who is actively miserable and not doing anything about it—but that was Matilda. And such was the state of our affairs when Hatty Hosmer knocked on my stage door in Boston. *(She is about to proceed with more confidences, when she sees Emma give her "the look." She assumes an air of wounded dignity.)* But there's no point in boring you with the details. One thing just led to another, and the next thing you know, Hatty was joining Matilda and myself in Rome that winter— *(To Emma.)* To study sculpting. *(To the audience.)* The whole thing was very innocent. *(Protesting to Emma, who has said something.)* It was! *(She starts to speak to the audience, but turns back to Emma.)* How would you know? You weren't even there! *(She rises, laughing. The joke has been on Emma.)*

Where was I? Rome… Yes, well, there had been one slight obstacle. Hatty's father, Hiram—but we all called him "Elizabeth." I can't remember now why we did that. *(Laughing.)* Well, anyway, "Elizabeth" was terrified at the thought of his daughter leaving him. I never met a more possessive man in my life. He had even built a little studio on the back of his house, just so that Hatty could stay home and be a little "sculptress." *(Soberly.)* Don't ever call Hatty a sculptress. *(She laughs.)*

Well, her father made us all promise that we would send Hatty back at the end of a year. That was twenty-five years ago, and Hatty is still in Rome. Well, Hiram had a fit and he cut off all the money. But Hatty had her revenge. Oh, yes, she had her revenge.

What she did was, she designed a monument in honor of a girl who had murdered her father—Beatrice Cenci. You don't know who that is, but, believe me, everybody in Rome knew about Beatrice Cenci. Her father had locked her up and raped and beaten her for years, and than she finally hired someone to murder him. Well, they arrested her, of course, and sentenced her to die—she was only seventeen—and the whole city was in an uproar, especially the women.

Well, Hatty's statue of Beatrice was something else. It was the most exquisitely beautiful female form I have ever seen—and I've seen a few. She has the girl lying on the stone slab of her prison cell, looking for all the world like an angel on a cloud—sleeping unmolested at last. And she has the sweetest little smile on her face. Hatty's statue of Beatrice has gone around the world now. Yes, it even went back to Boston, where Elizabeth could see it. Oh, yes, Hatty had the last word. She always does... She always does. *(Rallying.)* But the point of this whole story is how I met Emma. *(Turning toward the wings.)* You were hoping I'd forget. *(To audience.)* So, anyway, Matilda and Hatty and I moved to Rome. And then Hatty did what most young women do to older women who have helped them unstintingly and from the pure goodness of their hearts—she dumped me. And didn't Matilda just love that! Poor Matilda. She never could do anything on her own. She had to let Hatty use her in order to hurt me. So the two of them got together to act out their little melodrama for my benefit. *(Reflecting.)*

I have a horror of amateur theatricals, and so I booked a tour of England, leaving my little semi-retired Juliet to her understudy of a Romeo back in Italy. And, of course, after I left, there wasn't much point in the whole thing for Hatty, so she dumped Matilda. And then Matilda came running up to London, her little tail tucked between her legs, to see if I would take her back. I did, of course, but nothing could be the same between us—thanks to Hatty. But I had my revenge—*(Toward the wings.)* Didn't I? *(To audience.)* This is the good part.

Emma came over from the States to study sculpting, and of course, she met Hatty. Everybody who came to Rome had to see the Pope and Hatty. Not necessarily in that order. So, Emma met Hatty, and

because I was still under contract for another month, and, heaven knows, my notices certainly couldn't be any worse. So he told me the role of Lady Macbeth was mine if I wanted it. I wanted it.

Lady Macbeth. In two weeks. Now, bear in mind I was still just nineteen years old, and I had never performed a play in my life—much less a Shakespearean play, much less a lead role. But this was it—my one chance, and *I could not fail.*

What did I do? I made a plan. I would impersonate a famous actor who had been a success in the role. Not a bad plan—except that the actor I chose was Sarah Siddons. Sarah Siddons. "The" Sarah Siddons. England's greatest tragedienne. Lovely Sarah Siddons. Petite Sarah Siddons. Charming, seductive, gracious, vivacious, flirtatious, *feminine* Sarah Siddons. *(She nods.)* Yes, Sarah Siddons... *(A damsel in distress, veddy proper accent.)*

> *Alack, I am afraid they have awak'd,*
> *And 'tis not done; th' attempt, and not the deed,*
> *Confounds us. Hark! I laid their daggers ready,*
> *He could not miss 'em. Had he not resembled*
> *My father as he slept, I had done't.*

*(She laughs.)* The director was concerned. He told me to be more passionate. *(Properly petulant.)*

> *... Go get some water,*
> *And wash this filthy witness from your hand.*
> *Why did you bring these daggers from the place?*
> *They must lie there. Go carry them, and smear*
> *The sleepy grooms with blood... "*
> *Oh!*

*(CHARLOTTE gives a feminine cry of exasperation.)*

> *... Infirm of purpose!*
> *Give me the daggers!*

*(A long pause.)* We were days from opening. The director was tearing his hair out. Finally he stopped the rehearsal. He told me I had no talent, that I was wasting my time, that I would never have a career on the stage, and that all my dreams were ridiculous.

Well, I might have accepted that I couldn't act. I might even have accepted that I didn't have a future—but that my dreams were ridiculous...? What did he know about the dreams of a nineteen-year old girl? What did he know about my wanting to hold another woman in my arms, to feel her soft breasts pressed against mine, to kiss her on the lips, to wake up in the morning with her head resting tenderly on my shoulder? What did he know about my dreams of having enough money so that the woman I loved could live with me for the rest of my life, so that I could travel anywhere I wanted, dress any way I pleased, do anything I liked with anyone I chose? Ridiculous? No, my dreams were not ridiculous. They were beautiful, and this man had no right to make fun of them.

What did I do? I reared up on my hind legs like a beast who has been cornered. I showed him my fangs, and I showed him my claws. I backed that poor fellow into a wall, my fists waving in his face, and I tore into him. I let him know exactly what I thought of his arrogance, of his conceit, and of his "Shakespe-ah." I don't know what all I said, but I know that I said it. And when I was all through, shaking from head to toe, tears running down my face, waiting for him to fire me—do you know what he did? He clapped. The son-of-a-bitch stood there and clapped. And then he said: *(Whispering.)*"Do it just like that." *(Smiling.)* And I did. *(She turns her back, for a moment to get into character. During this speech, CHARLOTTE directs rage toward her body and the disease which is ravaging it— alluding to the mastectomy at the end.)*

> *... The raven himself is hoarse*
> *That croaks the fatal entrance of Duncan*
> *Under my battlements. Come, you spirits*
> *That tend on mortal thoughts, unsex me here,*
> *(CHARLOTTE clutches her breast.)*
> *And fill me from the crown to the toe top-full*
> *Of direst cruelty! Make thick my blood,*
> *Stop up th' access and passage to remorse,*
> *That no compunctious visitings of nature*
> *Shake my fell purpose, nor keep peace between*
> *Th' effect and it! Come to my woman's breasts,*
> *And take my milk for gall, you murth'ring   ministers,*
> *Wherever in your sightless substances*

*You wait on nature's mischief! Come, thick night,*
*And pall thee in the dunnest smoke of hell,*
*That my keen knife see not the wound it makes,*
*Nor heaven peep through the blanket of the dark*
*To cry, 'Hold, hold!'*

*(She collapses in the chair, out of breath and panting.)* I stopped the show... Stopped it cold... *(Struggling for breath.)* They loved me... They loved me! *(Unable to rally, she signals toward the wings.)* I think this would be a good time... for us to take a break... *(Lights fade, as CHARLOTTE rises with extreme difficulty to exit. Blackout.)*

## END OF ACT I

## ACT II

*Lights come up on the same set. CHARLOTTE enters. She has rallied during the intermission, and she paces the stage like an animal in a cage. Conscious that her time is running out, CHARLOTTE plays with a feverish energy bordering on delirium.*

CHARLOTTE:
> *'Tis now the very witching time of night,*
> *When churchyards yawn and hell itself breathes out*
> *Contagion to this world. Now could I drink hot blood,*
> *And do such bitter business as the day*
> *Would quake to look on.*

*(Smiling.)* Hamlet... Emma didn't think I'd make it back for the second half. *(To Emma.)* Did you? *(To audience.)* She didn't think I'd recover from my surgery either. I had a breast removed four years ago. One of the first operations of its kind ever performed... *(Pausing.)* A distinction which was not without disadvantages. *But,* I survived. *(To Emma.)* Didn't I? *(To audience.)* And here I am.

*(Turning suddenly to Emma.)* I'll tell you what, Emma—I'll make a bet with you. If I don't finish the show tonight, I'll cancel the rest of the tour and go home with you. How's that? *(To the audience.)* She likes that. *(To Emma.)* But, you have to agree, if I *do* finish the show, you will go with me to San Francisco. *(To the audience.)* I've always wanted to go there. They'd love me in San Francisco, don't you think? *(To Emma.)* Well, what do you say? Is it a deal? *(Rallying, she turns to the audience.)* You are the witnesses! Miss Emma Stebbins has just agreed to accompany Miss Charlotte Cushman on a tour to California and points west.

*(Turning toward Emma, who has apparently interrupted her.)* What? *(Irritated.)* Of course, I'm going to tell them about Rosalie. I said I would, didn't I? *(To the audience.)* You want to hear about my first girlfriend, don't you? I thought so.

Rosalie... Rosalie Sully. I was twenty-six and she was twenty-two. Would you like to know how I seduced her? Well, I sat absolutely

51

motionless for hours at a time and never said a word. You don't believe me? Her father was painting my portrait. *(She laughs.)* Rosalie Sully… *(Sitting.)* Well, Mother thought the whole thing was disgusting. She presented me with an ultimatum: Give up Rosalie or move out of the house… *(Defensive.)* What could I do? I was young, and I had no one to advise me. I did what I thought was the right thing. I felt I had no choice at the time… *(With mock contrition.)* I rented an apartment, so Rosie could sleep with me. *(Laughing heartily, she rises and crosses downstage.)* Oh, we were in love. We were so in love—and I had waited so long! Is there anything like that first girlfriend? It was sweet and tender and passionate and everything I had ever dreamed it would be. And more. And better. Rosalie Sully. My Rose. She died while I was over in England. Died at twenty-six… Beautiful Rose.

*(Changing the subject abruptly.)* But that reminds me—we were doing death this evening, weren't we? I suppose you want to see me die. That's what they pay me for. So—what's your pleasure? Suicide? Sword wound? Musket ball…? How about poison? Poison is good.

This is Hamlet's mother, Gertrude. She has to die in front of both her husband and her son, but without upstaging either one of them. Needless to say, this is a role which presents a challenge for many women.

*(CHARLOTTE, a vapid expression on her face, lifts the glass and sips from it as if it were wine. She suppresses a series of coughs, rises in alarm, only to lose her balance, and waves to Claudius to indicate that he is not to worry. Attempting to sit, she falls out of the chair and lies panting on the floor, but still indicates that there is nothing wrong. Pulling at the neck of her dress and gasping for air, she crawls painfully toward the front of the stage. She rejects an offer of help:)*

    *No, no…*
*(Gesturing toward the table.)*
    *… the drink, the drink—O my dear Hamlet—*
    *The drink, the drink! I am pois'ned.*

*(A final suppressed gasp—and a wave to her husband to indicate that he is not to worry—and Gertrude expires.)*

And then there's Queen Katharine. She dies of a broken heart. Henry the Eighth has divorced her, and this is her way of getting even. It takes her eight pages to die. *(Moving the chair center stage.)* I'll just hit the highlights. *(She positions herself by the chair.)*

> *My legs like loaden branches bow to th' earth,*
> *Willing to leave their burthen...*

*(Snapping her fingers.)*

> *... Reach a chair.*

*(She sits.)*

> *So; now, methinks, I feel a little ease.*

*(She begins to sink, but rouses herself, irritably snapping her fingers.)*

> *Patience —*

*(Coming out of character.)* Patience is her maid. *(Katharine again, snapping again.)*

> *Patience, be near me still, and set me lower;*
> *I have not long to trouble thee...*

*(Rousing herself and snapping her fingers.)*

> *Cause the musicians play me that sad note*
> *I nam'd my knell, whilst I sit meditating*
> *On that celestial harmony I go to.*

*(She sinks, but, irritated, she rallies for another snap.)*

> *... Bid the music leave,*
> *They are harsh and heavy to me*

*(Coming out of character and rising.)* Here's Patience: *(A long scream.)*

> *... How pale she looks,*
> *And of an earthy cold... Mark her eyes!*

*(Another scream, and then she is Katharine again, rolling her eyes. She starts to die, but rallies.)*

> *... Patience, is that letter*
> *I caus'd you write yet sent away?...*
> *... Sir, I most humbly pray you to deliver*
> *This to my lord the King...*

53

"I knew it would be like this!" *(Collapsing on the floor, she crawls the entire length of the stage to snatch victory from the jaws of defeat. She speaks her dying words to Dirk.)* "It has ended as it ought."

*(After dying a lugubrious death, CHARLOTTE rises and dusts herself off.)* Meg Merrilies, Queen of the Gypsies… But I didn't just play queens. I played princes and kings, too. Breeches parts. That's what they called it when we took the men's roles. And why shouldn't we? They had all the lines.

I played Aladdin, and Oberon—King of the Fairies… And two cardinals—Richelieu and Cardinal Wolsey. I was the first woman to play Cardinal Wolsey. And, of course, Hamlet. I borrowed Edwin Booth's costume. *(Remembering.)* Filled it out better than he did, too. *(She laughs.)* But my most famous breeches part was Romeo. Oh, Romeo! How I loved to play that boy! Mad, passionate, tempestuous Romeo. I loved him! I *was* Romeo! *(Shaking her head.)* All those years of pent-up passion for my girlfriends… All those long nights of fantasy—and frustration! I felt as if I had been rehearsing for Romeo all my life.

And Susan was my first Juliet. My baby sister Susan. You didn't know that, did you? Yes, my sister and I acted together for ten years. And those were the best years of my life. Especially, *Romeo and Juliet*, and especially when we took the play to London. Yes, Susan and I were a team. Top billing: "Charlotte Cushman and her sister."

Well, Mother had a fit. It was bad enough that *I* was in the theatre, but Susan! Oh, no, not Susan! —not her precious, little, blue-eyed, baby girl! No, Mother had it all planned out that her *beautiful* daughter was going to marry a rich man, and that he was going to support the whole family, and then she and Susan would never have to work again. *(A bitter laugh.)* And Mother was in such a hurry to spare Susan a life of drudgery, she forced her into marriage at the age of thirteen. Thirteen. How did she get Susan to go along with it? Well, she told her that the man was sick and going to die soon— which is what he had told Mother—and that the whole thing was just a legal formality so that Susan could inherit his property. Well, needless to say, the scoundrel was lying about the state of his finances— *and* his health! One year later, there was Susan, my baby sister, fourteen-year-old Susan—pregnant, abandoned, and being hounded by an army of creditors. Well, I came to the rescue, of course. I was already supporting Mother and both my brothers.

But I'll tell you something— the day—the very *day* that baby was weaned, I marched Susan down to the Park Theatre and got her an audition. My baby sister was *never* going to have to depend on a man again —not if I could help it!

Well, they cast her, and then Susan and I started working together. You know, the women didn't usually team up—but *we* did. We knew each other's timing, we knew each other's business—There was no one in the theatre who could beat us! And we played everything—*everything*: Mistress Page and Mistress Ford in *Merry Wives*, Gertrude and Ophelia in *Hamlet*, Oberon and Helena in *Midsummer Night's Dream*, Lydia Languish and Lucy in *The Rivals,* Desdemona and Emilia in *Othello*, Lady Macbeth and Lady Macduff, and then—our most daring—*Romeo and Juliet*!

In 1846 we took the show to London. Oh, that was a story! But first we thought it would be a good idea to try it out in Scotland. Well, we managed to scandalize the entire population of Edinburgh. For weeks rumors were flying that Susan was an unwed mother, and that I was... well, what I am!

Of course, none of this would hurt our reputations in London. No, what almost stopped us there was a dead actor. That's right, a dead actor. His name was David Garrick.

It seems that Mr. Garrick had taken it upon himself to improve on Shakespeare's plays—which meant, of course, writing longer scenes for himself and cutting the women's lines. Oh, do I know David Garrick! He may have died before I was born, but I know him. I have been sharing the stage now for forty years with the David Garricks of this world, and they are no different now than they were a hundred years ago.

Well, Mr. Garrick had done such an excellent job of promoting himself, that his version of *Romeo and Juliet* had become more popular than Shakespeare's. When Susan and I got to London to rehearse with the company at the Haymarket, there was not a single actor who knew the original version. Furthermore, they absolutely refused to learn it. No, they were not about to let two Americans teach them their Shakespeare—much less two women, much less a woman who intended to dress like a man and make love to her sister! *(Laughing.)* Well, Susan and I had no intention of performing the Garrick butchery—so there we were, on the verge of an actors' strike. Then, at the eleventh hour, the manager of the Haymarket stepped in. He posted a modest notice in the Green Room, to the effect that any actor who was not willing to cooperate with the Misses Cushman would be free to seek employment elsewhere.

And so we opened. December thirtieth, 1846. And we were an immediate sensation. I have always maintained that only a woman can play Romeo with any credibility. The male actors with the maturity and experience to handle the role are obviously too old to be boys. On the other hand, an experienced actress can impersonate a young man well into her forties—provided, of course, she has the right "attitude." *(To Emma.)* Then, too, there are those things that only a woman can know about what pleases a woman. *(To the audience.)* Apparently the critics agreed. They wrote that I put their gender to shame with my lovemaking. Yes, rumor had it that "Miss Cushman was a very dangerous young man." *(Laughing.)* So, Susan and I were a sensation. We ran for eighty consecutive performances at the Haymarket—which was a record. And then we went on tour to the provinces. And then Susan had to go and ruin it all. She got married... again! *(CHARLOTTE begins to pace.)* Helena, *Midsummer Night's Dream.*

> *Injurious Hermia, most ungrateful maid!*
> *Have you conspir'd, have you with these contriv'd*
> *To bait me with this foul derision?*
> *Is all the counsel that we two have shar'd,*
> *The sisters' vows, the hours that we have spent,*
> *When we have chid the hasty-footed time*
> *For parting us—O, is all forgot?*
> *All school-days friendship,childhood innocence?*

*We, Hermia, like two artificial gods,*
*Have with our needles created both one flower,*
*Both on one sampler, sitting on one cushion,*
*Both warbling of one song, both in one key;*
*As if our hands, our sides, voices, and minds*
*Had been incorporate. So we grew together,*
*Like a double cherry, seeming parted,*
*But yet an union in partition,*
*Two lovely berries molded on one stem;*
*So, with two seeming bodies, but one heart...*
*(With sudden fury.)*
*... And will you rent our ancient love asunder,*
*To join with men in scorning your poor friend?*
*It is not friendly, 'tis not maidenly.*
*Our sex, as well as I, may chide you for it,*
*Though I alone do feel the injury.*

Yes, Susan got married. She got married and gave up acting. Or I should say, she gave up the stage. Her whole marriage was a performance, if you ask me. We were never close again after that. *(Agitated by her memories.)* Yes, Susan betrayed me. Just like Matilda. Just like Hatty. Just like all the women I have tried to love—they always leave me. I don't understand it. I have never abandoned a woman in my life. *(Turning with irritation toward Emma who has interrupted her.)* What? *(In a threatening tone.)* What about Rosalie? *(Pause.)* I told them she died. *(Bullying the audience.)* Didn't I? I told you she died while I was in England, didn't I? *(To Emma.)* See? I told them... *(She starts to address the audiences, but turns back to Emma with sudden ferocity.)* But you want me to say I murdered her, don't you? Stuck a knife in her heart like Iago—don't you? That I betrayed her, because I told her I would only be gone for six months, and instead, I stayed in England for three years.

*(With rising anger.)* Yes, I did stay. Because for the first time in my life I was a leading lady. For the first time in my life the managers were coming to *me*. And for the first time in my life, money—*real* money—was finally coming in. And wasn't that the whole point? To make enough money so that Rosie and I could live together for the rest of our lives? Yes, I stayed, and I would do it again.

truth was, I had outgrown Rosalie. How could I tell her that? But I never should have lied to her. That was the betrayal. Rosie deserved the truth. We all deserve the truth.

*(Looking at Emma.)* Well, Emma... it looks like you've won the bet. *(She begins to gather the books.)* You know, the great tragedy of *Romeo and Juliet* is that Romeo doesn't know that Juliet is still alive. He puts himself through all that agony for nothing. All the time Juliet is just waiting for him... waiting for him, and he doesn't have the sense to know it.

*(A long look at Emma.)* Well— *(She rises. This is her farewell to forty years      in the theatre.)*

> Our revels now are ended. These our actors
> *(As foretold you)* were all spirits, and
> Are melted into air, into thin air,
> And, like the baseless fabric of this vision,
> The cloud-capp'd tow'rs, the gorgeous palaces,
> The solemn temples, the great globe itself,
> Yea, all which it inherit, shall dissolve,
> And like this insubstantial pageant faded
> Leave not a rack behind. We are such stuff
> As dreams are made on; and our little life...

*(Pausing to smile.)*

> ... Is rounded with a sleep.

*(To Emma.)* Let's go home, Emma. I'm tired. *(To the audience.)* Goodnight. *(Exiting with tremendous dignity.)*

**BLACKOUT**

**END OF PLAY**

# CALAMITY JANE SENDS A MESSAGE

# TO HER DAUGHTER

**SYNOPSIS:**

Calamity Jane, a cross-dressing, masculine woman in the late stages of alcoholism, alternates between charming and alienating her audience as she attempts to legitimize her legacy by claiming to have been Bill Hickok's true love, as well as the mother of his child. A rough-rider, soldier, and stagecoach driver, Calamity is discovering that her gender deviancy is causing her to be erased from history at a time when her male comrades are becoming enshrined as legends.

*Calamity Jane Sends A Message to Her Daughter* is a tribute to masculine women living in times when lesbian or transgendered identities were not understood.   Accustomed to ridicule and contempt, Calamity survives through a combination of self-deprecating   humor,   myth-making,   and   alcohol—shrewdly propagating the myths about herself that will ensure her a place in history.

One woman
15 minutes
Single set

## CAST OF CHARACTERS

CALAMITY JANE: An old, alcoholic bag lady, masculine in appearance.

SCENE: A hall or theatre.

TIME: 1903.

# CALAMITY JANE SENDS A MESSAGE TO HER DAUGHTER

*There is a simple wooden bench on the stage and next to it, a spittoon. CALAMITY JANE enters from the side. She is in her late forties. In spite of her debauched appearance and poor physical condition, she exudes an irrepressible vitality of spirit. She wears a faded shirt, filthy jeans, and long johns, visible under the shirt. She wears a battered felt hat with a brim.*

*She crosses to the bench and dumps her body onto it. She hitches up her pants and spreads her legs, getting comfortable. A deep gutteral vibration, which seems to originate in her gut, moves up her chest and into her throat, culminating in a wad of phlegm, which CALAMITY, the expert markswoman, aims into the spittoon. She sits back and looks, for the first time, directly at the audience.*

CALAMITY: Kinda makes ya sick, don't it? *(She looks over the audience.)* You didn't expect me to swaller it, did you? *(Apparently they did. JANE grabs the spittoon and tips it in their direction.)* Look! *(She holds up it and rotates it so that the contents will be visible to every person in the room.)* Now you tell me how it's more ladylike to swaller a thing like that than to spit it out. *(Satisfied that she's made her point, she puts the spittoon back, with a snort of disgust:)* Ladies.

*(JANE sits back on the bench and regards her audience slowly and comprehensively, looking them right in the eye. When she is finished with her inventory, she sums up the sorry results:)* Well, you're certainly not men. *(Resigning herself, she begins to roll her sleeves.)*

I come here tonight 'cause I want to give y'all a message to take to muh Janey for me. I can tell you know her. *(Looking up briefly.)* She looks like one of y'all. *(Suddenly, she reaches up under her seat and yanks at the crotch of her pants.)* Muh union suit's gettin' fresh with me. *(She settles herself back on the bench.)* Janey's muh daughter. I ain't seen her since she was a little girl. I give her up.

*(She pauses, judging the reaction to this information.)* Yep. Give her up like liquor an' tabaccy.

*(She snorts, enjoying her little joke, and then becomes suddenly remorseful.)* Naw, that ain't so... *(A mischievous look.)* I still chew! *(She really knocks herself out with this one, and her paroxysm develops into a coughing fit, ending with another wad of phlegm landing in the spittoon. She responds to the audience with defiance.)*

Janey's a lady. Swallers her spit. Yep, they raised her real good. *(Pausing.)* I give her to folks who had a lot of money. *(She reaches for her flask or bottle of whiskey and begins to unscrew the top.)* Anyway, I got a couple of things I want you to tell her for me. Things she oughtta know about her mother. *(Jane takes a slug of whiskey, which is apparently very strong. She considers the audience's response to her drinking.)* I drink for my eyes. *(A serious pause, followed by a mischievous aside:)* Helps me close 'em! *(She explodes into laughter, coughing as she sets the bottle down. She returns to her subject.)*

First off, she don't know I'm her mother. You might want to set her down for that one. Kinda like findin' out you're pregnant, only backwards. So go easy on her. Get her broke to the saddle first. *(A pause, as anger begins to creep into her voice.)* Maybe tell her that her mama ain't dead like they told her. *(Another thoughtful pause.)* An' then tell her that her mother lives out in Wyoming. *(Another pause.)* An' then say how much her mama loves animals. *(She reaches for the bottle again and unscrews the top, not looking at the audience.)* An' then you can just natcherly ease into the part about muleskinnin' an' bullwhackin.' *(She looks up mischievously.)* An' then show her muh pitcher! *(She winks, laughs, and takes a slug of whiskey.)* Sure hope she drinks... *(She sets the bottle down, serious again.)*

Her real name is Jane Canarray Hickok. That's "Hickok," as in "Wild Bill." We was married, and don't you let anyone tell you different. We was married. He was muh man. Me an' Bill, just like that... *(She holds two fingers together.)* An' Janey's his daughter. You tell her. *(She looks away.)*

Bill was a man. A real man. *(Turning to the audience, with sudden accusatory anger.)* Not one of your lily-livered, pasty-faced, limp-dick farmer types! *(Backing off just as suddenly.)* Nope. Bill was *every inch* a man. "Inch," hell... *(Mischievous.)* Every *foot* a man! *(She explodes into laughter and coughing. After a moment she collects herself.)* I met Bill when I was still wet behind the ears. Just a kid. See I was orphaned when I was fourteen, and I learned to hustle pretty good... *(To herself.)* Had to. *(After a pause, she turns back to the audience.)*

First time we met, we was in a poker game together, an' I beat him. I beat him real bad. Bill don't like to lose, 'specially with folks watchin,' so he rears up an' calls me a cheater. So I says... *(Slowly, savoring the moment.)* "Hickok, you play cards so dumb I'd have to cheat to lose!" *(Smiling.)* Well... everybody's laughin' at that one, so he pulls out his gun, an' then Molly behind the bar yells out... *(Imitating a shrill female voice.)* "Put that back, Bill! That there's a gal!"

*(Smiling.)* Well, that done it! He just stands there lookin' at me like a hog starin' at a wristwatch. An' then all of a sudden he throws his gun on the table an' hollers, "Drinks for the house...!" *(Hoisting the bottle.)* "I want all of ya'll to drink to this here gal—the finest poker player in the Territories!" *(She drinks a toast to herself. She savors the memory for a moment and then sets the bottle down before returning to her narrative.)*

Bill took a shine to me, an' we started keepin' each other company. *(Musing, deep in her memories.)* Come spring we headed south down towards Abilene, an' we started workin' the border. *(Looking up suddenly.)* I was his partner. Called muhself "Jack of Diamonds." Between the two of us, we hustled a wagonload of money. *(Back in her own thoughts again.)* Pissed it away, too. An' all that time nobody knowed I was a woman... *(Looking up suddenly again.)* 'Cept Bill. *(To herself.)* He knowed it all right. *(To the audience.)* I got pregnant, but I didn't want Bill to know. So I told him I was restless, an' I took off by myself up the trail to Yellowstone Valley, up to a place called Benson's Landin.' *(She reaches for the bottle and begins to unscrew the top.)* Benson's Landin' ain't there no more. They got themselves a town called Livingston instead... *(She*

69

*snorts and shakes her head in disgust at the pretension.)*
"Livingston... " *(She takes a long drink. This is a painful memory,
and she holds tight to the bottle as she tells it.)*

I had that baby in the dead of winter, all by myself, and I swole up
like a pig after it, and I was runnin' a fever so high, I throwed the
blankets off, with the water froze in the bucket right next to me! An'
if misery ain't hell, I run outta liquor. *(Another long pause, before
she collects herself.)* I says to ole Janey, "It's every man for
himself." Didn't figger either one of us was gonna make it. *(She sets
the bottle down and takes off her hat. Underneath it,   her hair is
short, dirty, and slicked back. It's a man's haircut. She turns the hat
in her hand as she speaks.)*

I reckon it was about two days after I had that baby that Cap'n
O'Neil knocks on the door of the cabin. He come lookin' to find the
grave of his brother, killed somewhere around there by the injuns.
*(Looking up.)* The Sioux. *(Looking down at the hat again.)* They
bothered everybody around there 'cept me. They thought I was
crazy. Don't know what I ever done to give 'em that idea. *(She
pauses, considers, and puts the hat back on her head with a sigh of
resignation.)* Well, anyway, I told this cap'n that I didn't know
nothing 'bout his brother's grave, but if he cared to come back in a
week, he could take a look at mine. I guess he figgered that was
about the size of things, 'cause he went and got us some wood, and
cooked me some food, and he bought me some whiskey, too. An' if
good whiskey can't save ya, then you're already dead. *(She picks up
the bottle and takes a drink. After a moment, she looks away and
begins to speak. She does not look a the audience.)*

This O'Neil fella, he took to Janey. Started talkin' 'bout how him
an' his wife couldn't have no babies, and how he would take Janey
to England, get her some proper schoolin,' playin' a piano and
speakin' languages and all that stuff... *(She turns back to the
audience.)* Mostly, though, I was thinkin' 'bout what would happen
to Janey if I died, seein's how I almost just did. Nobody was gonna
want her. Some family'd take her to keep like some kind of slave or
somethin' and then when she was twelve or fourteen, she'd prob'ly
head out on her own like I done, an' that ain't no life for anybody.

*(Looking away.)* So when she was a year old, the cap'n come back, and I give her to him.

*(To the audience, with painful vulnerability)* You tell Janey I was nineteen, an' I thought I was doin' the right thing. *(With sudden ferocity.)* You tell her, and you tell anybody else who asks you that I *still* say I done the right thing! *(Closing her eyes to collect herself.)*

But that ain't the point... *(She opens her eyes.)* I was talkin' about Wild Bill... *(Sudden focus on being factual.)* I didn't see him again 'til two years later. By then I was livin' in Deadwood... '76. It was the summer of '76. I remember I was havin' a beer in Russell's saloon. I was the only woman in Deadwood they let in that saloon. Anyway, I had just stepped outside to talk to a buddy of mine, and I look up Main Street, and I think I'm dreamin' or somethin.' *(A slow grin spreads over her face. She is reliving the moment.)*

Here comes Bill, ridin' his horse, him and Colorado Charlie and Bloody Dan Seymour. They come ridin' down Main Street. And they was all wearin' bran' new *white* Stetsons, fringed buckskins, and shiney boots. And they had so much silver on their saddles it was hard on your eyes to look at 'em. We went to every saloon in town that afternoon, an' the sight of Bill was so purty next to me, I shot out all the mirrors! *(She stands suddenly, her palms together as if they were holding a pistol, and mimes the shooting. She does a little jig step, laughing at the memory, and then, satisfied, sits back on the bench.)*

That is what I think of when I think of Bill... That summer, an' him ridin' down Main Street into Deadwood. *(She grunts and reaches for the bottle.)* End of that summer, he got killed. Sonofabitch McCall. Shot him from behind. *(She raises the bottle as a salute.)* Bill. He was a man. Not like that McCall.

*(She takes a long drink, followed by a thoughtful pause.)* Bill *always* shot 'em from the front. *(Her face softens, as she strokes the side of her face with the bottle.)* Had them long, stallion-tail mustaches down the sides of his face. Bill was my man. We was just like that, me an' Bill... *(She holds her two fingers together.)* Just like that.

71

*(She shows us again.)* Don't care what people tell you. I know. *(She sets the bottle down. She is now visibly drunk.)*

Them preacher's daughter types was always throwin' themselves at Bill, but they couldn't understand him. Hell, what'd they know about his life? *(She lurches off the bench and crosses down right.)* Me, I drove a stagecoach, I fought the injuns, I rode with the cavalry... till they caught me takin' a bath. *(An aside.)* Let *that* be a lesson to you... *(Crossing down left.)* Hell... I *laid rail*. I done everything a man's done, and maybe more. I knowed what Bill was thinkin' before he said it. I understood him. Wasn't anybody understood him better than me. *(With increasing anger and erratic movement.)*

I want Janey to know that when people try to tell her he already had a wife, that is pure *hog slop*! Bill's wife was me! Back east he went through some tin-whistle ceremony with this lady who owned a circus, but he only done it to get himself a job, that's all. Business. That's all it was. Had a good head for business. But I was his woman. And Janey's his daughter. *(Pausing to recollect her argument.)*

The reason I ain't never told nobody is that things kinda creep up on ya when ya get older. *(She retrieves the bottle.)* Back then, we was just roughnecks on a toot. But times has changed now. Bill Hickok's in all the books. I want Janey to know she come from somebody famous. *(She takes a drink.)* Her mama may have been a no-count drunk nobody, but her daddy was somebody. *(A pause. She muses to herself with sudden hostility.)* He was *some*body all right... *(Looking up quickly with a drunken smile.)* I'm gonna be buried next to Bill. *(She sits. Very drunk, she appears to have lost her train of thought. She takes an uncomfortably long pause before resuming her narrative. When she does, it is barely coherent.)*

A man don't always go for looks, ya know... He got his outside and his inside. A man don't always know he got an inside. But I know. I seen Bill's inside and his inside seen me. So I didn't never let his outside self bother me too much. Because I knowed more about him than he knowed about himself. And I know he loved me. An' he woulda loved Janey too, if he'd ever seen her. Yeah, the three of us would have been a pair. *(She shows us the two fingers again. She grunts and takes a long pause. It appears that she may be about to fall asleep, and when she speaks, it is to herself.)*

Anyway, I done a lot of things in muh life that Janey wouldn't understand. Hell, I don't understand. *(Noticing the audience again.)* But I ain't all as bad as they make out, either. *(A pause.)* You ask who midwifed half the babies in Deadwood. *(This triggers a memory, and she suddenly rallies and becomes very animated.)* You ask who nursed them folks with smallpox when not one *single soul* would set foot in the pest house, except yours truly. *(With acute pain.)* Them women all the time actin' uppity-up 'cause I don't look all frilly and smell like roses, but... *(Speaking very slowly and deliberately.)*... you ask 'em if they wasn't damn glad *I didn't* care what muh face looked like when they was needin' somebody to nurse 'em through smallpox! *(She leans toward the audience and spits her words at them.) Ast 'em! (A pause. She sits back.)*

You tell Janey her mother done some good things. Done some bad ones too. *(Suddenly mischievous.)* Sometimes you catch the chicken and sometimes you jes' git the feathers! *(Her laughter triggers a coughing spell, and she slides into self-pity and resentment again, her speech noticeably slurred.)* But you tell her that whatever people say about her mother, she can hold her head up high, 'cause her daddy was *James... Butler... Hickok!* *(She spits out his name out in a mixture of defiance and hostility. Rising, she pauses for a moment to get her bearings, and then retrieves her bottle, and starts to exit. She accidentally stumbles into the spittoon, and spins around to see if someone has attacked her. Realizing it was the spittoon, she turns abruptly and lurches off the stage.)*

**BLACKOUT**

**END OF PLAY**

73

# COOKIN' WITH TYPHOID MARY

**SYNOPSIS:**

Mary Mallon, dubbed "Typhoid Mary" by a hostile press, never admitted that she was a typhoid carrier. Her persistent refusal to defer to medical experts infuriated George Soper, a sanitation engineer for New York City. He built his career on tracking down Mary and incarcerating her. In this monologue, Mary speaks for herself. An Irish emigrant, she traces the story of her persecution back to the Potato Famine, all the while cutting out the eyes of the potatoes and chopping them for the stew pot in the kitchen of the mysterious institution where she has found employment under a false name.

Mary's version of events is both humorous and chilling. She resists a theory that would indict her as a carrier of invisible agents of death, when half the population of Ireland starved to death in plain view before the eyes of an indifferent world.

One woman
25 minutes
Single set

# CAST OF CHARACTERS

MARY MALLON: A physically imposing, working-class Irish
  woman.

SCENE: A industrial kitchen.

TIME: 1914.

# COOKIN' WITH TYPHOID MARY

*The scene is a large, but shabby institutional kitchen. In the center of the stage is a long table with a cutting board and a huge institutional cooking pot. There are sacks of potatoes, onions, and tomatoes scattered on the table and the floor surrounding it. A tall stool stands to one side of the table.*

*MARY MALLON is cooking. MARY is a physically imposing Irish woman of forty-five. She wears a cheap dress from 1914, with a soiled apron over it. As the play opens, MARY is chopping a potato to throw in the pot. She uses an enormous knife, and sings while she works:*

MARY: *(Singing:)*
  WE HAVE A LOYAL LITTLE FRIEND
  THE POTATO SMOOTH AND ROUND,
  AND SELDOM DOES IT FAIL TO LEND,
  A DISH THAT'S GOOD AND SOUND...

*(MARY stops abruptly, noticing the audience.)* There wouldn't be a George Soper here, would there? A "Doctor" George Soper? Nasty little pig-eyed bastard holdin' his hat over his privates like he's got somethin' to be ashamed of, which he does! *(Looking around,)* No? Well, if he comes in, you'll tell me, won't you? I've got a little present for him. *(She picks up the large knife again and resumes chopping.)*

And you don't need to be starin' at me like you don't know who I am. Mary Mallon. Mary Mallon of Tuxedo Park, Oyster Island, Park Avenue and Riverside. Don't tell me you never heard the name? Mary Mallon. The finest cook in Manhattan. The one they all ask for when they go to the agencies. That's me. Mary Mallon. *(She lifts the knife to chop a potato, but stops in mid-swing to inspect it.)*

Now, you don't want to be cuttin' this one. See how green the end is? That means it wasn't deep enough in the ground. You've got to bury them good while they're young, or they turn out bitter, don't you know? *(She tosses it to the side.)*

So you're askin' yourself what a fine woman like Mary Mallon is doin' in this dungeon of a kitchen, slavin' away at a pile of potatoes, and only herself to be doin' the work of a dozen. You're askin' yourself who's responsible for her bein' in this hell-hole, and I'll tell you. It was that devil of a doctor, George Soper. Him and his hat and what's under it. *(She chops with a vengeance and picks up the pieces to throw in the pot, when suddenly something on one of the pieces catches her eye.)*

Will you look at this! Eyes as big as a baby's finger. *(She begins to "eye" the potato pieces.)* Them eyes is really sprouts, you know. If you have a potato long enough, them little eyes grows hands and starts feelin' their way towards the light, and then you've got trouble. One day you open up the cabinet for your sack of potatoes, and there they are—hundreds of gropin' little pale hands, stretchin' themselves out to you, just beggin' for a touch of sunlight. And you can't have that! *(She whacks the cutting board with the knife, and then laughs at her own violence.)* It takes food to be growin' them little hands. You can't be lettin' them little eyes see too much, or the next thing you know they'll be stealing the potato for themselves, instead of leavin' it for them that paid for it, the way God meant it to be. So you've got to poke them out—like this. *(She gouges a potato eye with her knife.)*

Now, if I was cookin' for them rich folks still, I'd be peelin' the skins off, too. That's how them rich folks like their potatoes—all pale and smooth, like them pictures of naked women they got hangin' on their walls. Like they was made up in heaven by God himself and flown to earth by the angels. Like a potato didn't come up out of the ground rough and dirty like them that dug it up. They don't like to think about things like that, them rich folks. And why should they? They're never goin' to look down on that fancy silver platter and see a potato sittin' there, black with blight, crumblin' to pieces when you touch it, like a rotten tooth in an old man's head. *(She whacks another potato and begins to sing:)*

WE HAVE A LOYAL LITTLE FRIEND
THE POTATO SMOOTH AND ROUND,
AND SELDOM DOES IT FAIL TO LEND,
A DISH THAT'S GOOD AND SOUND.

OH! TRULY TIS A FRIEND IN NEED
THO TREATED WITH DISDAIN,
A MOST ESSENTIAL FOOD INDEED,
THAT FULLY EARNS ITS FAME.

My mother taught me that. She was from Galway. *(She inspects a potato.)* Galway was the worst, you know. She said there wasn't a single potato in the whole county that didn't have the blight. That was in '49. She said they was eatin' 'em anyway, black spots and all. But then, a rotten potato's not such a bad thing when you're cookin' up grass and seaweed to keep yourself alive. You see, there wasn't any grain or livestock left, because our landlords had come all the way over from England—in the spirit of Christian charity, don't you know—just to buy us out... *(Turning her attention back to the potato.)* Not that we weren't dyin' to sell. *(She chops it.)*

She was a fierce one, my mother. Told my da he could go to hell or stay in Dublin—it was all the same to her, but she was takin' her daughter where there was more to live for than watchin' your babies starve while you worked yourself to death. I never saw my da again—not that I'd have known it if I stepped on him. My mother borrowed the money to buy us a passage in steerage—just her and myself. And that's how we left, just the two of us. *(She takes out an onion and begins to peel it.)*

Well, she took sick on the crossin.' We all did. All of us that was in steerage. First you get the fever, and then you get the cramps, and then you go to passin' blood, and then you die—unless you live, which is just as bad as dyin' if you're down in steerage. And then they come and fetch your body and heave it over the side, like it was a sack of potatoes. Only, of course, they'd never throw a perfectly fine sack of potatoes into the water. *(She laughs.)* There's nothing to bring a tear to Mary Mallon's eye like an onion! *(She wipes her eyes and chops the onion.)*

But I was tellin' you about the crossin'. We both took sick together, and there we lay, the two of us, under the blankets, shiverin' and crampin' and wishin' we were rich enough to be makin' the crossin' in one of them heated cabins with a bed and a toilet and running water like them folks that leaned over the railin's in the daytime and tossed oranges at us like we were animals in a pit. And then one night, I'm lyin' with my mother and listenin' to the wailin' of a baby and thinkin' what a blessin' that it still had the strength to cry—when all of a sudden my mother grabs at me and starts openin' her mouth, and then just as sudden she closes it again, and she drops back beside me, and I ask her what she's seen, but she's not sayin' anything to me, and I feel her fingers lettin' go of my arm, so now it's me that's grabbin' onto her—and she's not movin' at all. She's not sayin' a word. Not makin' a bloody sound. And then I start to feel her legs against my feet, gettin' colder and colder. *(She wipes her eyes from the onions.)* So, what do I do? I start hailin' Mary, full of grace, that's what I do. *(She laughs.)* And when that doesn't work, I hail her again, and then again, and again! And you know, that's how they found us. My mother stiff as a poker, and dead for two days, and me clingin' to her like a barnacle and saying my Hail Mary's like I'm racing the devil to beat her to heaven. *(She laughs again.)*

Well, they had a time of it, gettin' her body. They sent down the ship's doctor, don't you know. And the only time the bastard ever set foot in steerage, was to come down and count up the dead. And here he is leanin' over me, tryin' to get a peek at my poor mother's face—and I jump on him like a cat guardin' her kittens, scratchin' and clawin' at his pasty white face, just tryin' to see what he would be lookin' like when he was dead! *(She laughs.)* It took 'em four men to fetch my mother's body—and three of them was just to get me off the doctor. *(She resumes chopping the onion.)* Of course, I lied about my age when we landed. I wasn't about to give them another chance to be feedin' Mary Mallon's body to the seagulls. *(She stops and looks at the audience.)* So now you're askin' yourself how a little girl, without a penny in her purse and not knowin' a livin' soul on the continent, managed to keep herself from starvin' to death. Well, you figure it out. You'd be surprised how much work there is for a little girl in New York. *(She throws the onion in the pot.)*

He hasn't come in, has he? That devil of a doctor, Soper...? You will tell me, if he comes in now? *(She pulls a tomato out of one of the sacks.)* You know the secret of cuttin' tomatoes? You slide the tip of the blade up under the skin just before you cut, and that way it won't spit the juice all over you. *(She begins to slice tomatoes. She becomes more and more aggressive, reducing the tomatoes to a mound of red pulp.)*

You know, people used to believe tomatoes was poison. I read it in the paper. It took a hundred years for some brave soul to get up the courage to eat one. Can you imagine it? Thinkin' a tomato was poison! Now, I ask you, what would give a body an idea like that about a tomato? Well, I'll tell you. Some poor woman cooked up a tomato one day, and then some rich old bastard had it for his dinner, and died in his sleep on account of his sins, and then don't you know, they go lookin' for the cook who must have done him in, because rich folks don't like to believe they have to die same as the poor and that for all their money, they can't bribe their way out of death like they can out of prison. No, they can't believe that, so they have to go out and find somebody to pin it on. And like as not the woman's Irish. And there you are—tomatoes are poison. And the next thing you know, it's in all the papers, and they start callin' her Tomato Mary. And then there's a dozen folks from all over New York, who suddenly remember hirin' a cook whose name was Mary, and that somebody somewhere died sometime after eatin' at their table. And then the whole world is hearin' of New York's tomato epidemic. And that poor woman's spendin' her life in hidin' or in jail for the ignorance and arrogance of the bloody rich who think they can buy their way out of everything. Well, just maybe it wasn't the tomatoes killed them. Maybe it was their own wretched lies pilin' up on their souls till they collapse in on them like a roof on rotted timbers. *(She grabs handfuls of the tomato pulp and dumps them into the pot as she sings:)*

THEY SAY SIR WALTER RALEIGH
(SO IT'S GENERALLY AGREED)
IMPLANTED IN OUR VALLEYS FAIR
THE FIRST PROLIFIC SEED.
THERE SPRANG FROM FERTILE SOIL
(AT LEAST THAT'S WHAT WE'RE TOLD)
WITH EAGER CARE AND EARNEST TOIL
A CROP A HUNDRED-FOLD

*(She goes back to chopping potatoes.)* Sir Walter Raleigh. He would be an Englishman, now, wouldn't he? A gentleman, too. And, look, he's bringin' a little souvenir from America over to Ireland! Now, isn't that kind of him, to be thinkin' of his neighbors and bringin' them the marvelous little potato? They say you can grow six wagonloads on one acre! And they say you can grow it in any kind of dirt! Now, isn't that a wonder? And why should a body be wastin' time and trouble with the likes of sheep, when for half the land and twice the money, you can be growin' the marvelous potato? So now all of Ireland starts sellin' off their land in great chunks and breedin' themselves like prize bulls, until there's four times the people livin' on twice the farms, if you can call five acres a farm. *(She becomes increasingly frenzied with her chopping as she speaks.)*

Ah, the marvelous potato. "Sir" Walter Raleigh never told us the potato would fail. He never told us it would fail five years in a row. He never told us he was bringin' death to Ireland, sowin' potatoes in the ground like they was the dragon's teeth in the story, and that everywhere he planted one, there would be springin' up a skeleton until Ireland was a land of corpses. No, he never told us that, did he? I'm sure "Sir" Walter Raleigh never dreamed his little potato was goin' to invade the Irish like a murderin' army of heathens—now did he? I'm sure no one ever accused him of killin' a single person, did they? I'm sure they never tried to lock him up for bein' a "potato carrier." But then, he was an Englishman, wasn't he? *(She wipes her hands on her apron, collecting herself.)*

You know I'm not usin' my real name here. I'm goin' by "Mary Brown." They're not goin' to find me here. Soper can look as hard as he wants, but he's never goin' to find me. I've picked the best place to hide in New York. *(She crosses down to the stool.)*

Soper—and a slimier little bastard you never saw. First time I laid eyes on him, he's standin' in the kitchen where I was workin'—got someone to show him in, the weasel did, and he's standin' there with his hat in his hand, in front of him like this, you know. You know how them gents do that. Hold it right here like they've got something to hide—which most of them do. And he calls out "Mary." And I look up like it should be someone that knows me, either that or someone who's hired me. But instead, I see this nasty little bastard— him and his little piggy eyes. And he's tellin' me he's from the city health department. And then he starts talkin' about little invisible animals, and I'm thinkin' it's on account of my bein' Irish—you know, the "little people," and all. So I tell Dr. Soper I'm a busy woman and if he'll get along with his business, then I'll be gettin' along with mine. Do you know what he does then? He looks me square in the eye and says, "Mary!"—not "Miss Mallon, mind you, but "Mary!" He says, "Mary! I want your blood, your urine, and your feces." Stood right there in the kitchen, he did, and said just like he was goin' over the menu. "Your blood, your urine, and your feces." And then he takes a step towards me, so I grab up the carvin' fork, like this... *(She demonstrates with the knife.)*... and I let him know what I think of him and his filthy mouth. I guess he sees who's goin' to be gettin' whose blood if it came to that, because he takes off runnin' down the hall, out the door, through the gate, and off down the sidewalk. You watch 'em when they hold their hats like that. *(She sets the knife down.)*

Now, you'd think that would be the end of Dr. Soper, but there's some of them that's been at their business so long, they've got no shame. He tracks me 'round to my roomin' house. I was livin' on Third Avenue, you know, there below 33rd Street. It was a decent place, I'll have you know. And this Soper, he's got a friend with him, and the two of them are waitin' on the landin' for, at the top of the stairs, talkin' loud enough for all the tenants in the buildin' to hear, and this time he asks me if I'm in the habit of washin' my hands after I go to the toilet! *(She returns to chopping her potatoes.)*

If you're a woman and you're Irish, they think they can say anything they like, and you've got to take it. Not this woman. Not Mary Mallon. I haven't lived through what I've lived through to be subjectin' myself to that kind of filth. I let the whole roomin' house know what I thought of that pair! Well, now, don't you see, I've humiliated him in front of his friend. Now he's goin' to be havin' to arrest me. *(Crossing back to the stool.)* But does he do his own dirty work? Not his kind! No, he goes out and gets himself a woman for the job. A Dr. S. Josephine Baker. And a fine one she was—wearin' a jacket and a tie like she was a man. Had her hair all combed back like one, too. *(MARY shakes her head.)*

She was a tricky one. The first time I found out her business, I slammed the door in her face. So then she comes back, her and three police officers. And this time, she goes around to the servant's entrance in the basement and rings the bell, so I won't suspect it was them. As soon as I see who it is, I try to slam the door, but one of the police has already got his bloody foot in the door. So I run back upstairs, and here's another peeler at the front door! So I go back to the kitchen and climb out the window. There's a fence between this house and the one next to it, so I pull a chair to it and climb over. And there's a little shed built into the back of the house, so I go in there and hide, pullin' the ash cans to the door, so they won't suspect I'm in there. So here's poor Mary Mallon, crouchin' for three hours in the freezin' cold, no jacket—and just when I'm thinkin' it might be safe to come out, that bloodhound of a doctor spots a bit of my dress from under the door. And they come after me—her and the three peelers. Well, I give them a run for their money—just like I done on that ship—kickin' and bitin' even after they get my arms pinned back. Kicked one of them peelers so hard, he said his equipment would never work again! *(She chops a potato.)*

Well, don't you know, they've hired an ambulance so it looks like they're public officials doin' their duty by takin' a poor crazy woman away, instead of criminals kidnappin' an honest citizen on account of that dirty-minded bastard Soper. And Dr. S. Josephine Baker—she was sittin' on top of me the whole ride! *(Chopping again.)*

And they lock me in a hospital room. It's like a peeled potato, this room is. White walls, white ceiling, white floor. And they take my clothes and they give me a white bathrobe. And they keep checkin' the bedpan every few hours. I know what they want. Didn't that bastard Soper stand right there and tell me to my face? I've seen his kind. So I'm tryin' not to oblige, but nature's not friendly. And of course, they come and take the pot away now. So then after I'm in this hell-hole for a while, the little bastard himself decides to show himself. He comes in and stands in front of the door, in case he might have to leave in a hurry. So, he's standin' like this with his back to the door. And he's talkin' to me like I'm a misbehavin' child and he's my da, and that I've done somethin' he ought to

86

forgive me for. He's goin' on about them invisible things again—only now he's more excited, because he's got what he wanted from me, and he's tellin' me the invisible things is crawlin' all over—and he tells me that when I go to the toilet, they crawl up my hands and then, if I don't wash them off, they crawl onto the food and people eat them and die! And then he gets onto what really excites him—my gall bladder. So then I know the bastard intends to murder me. He tells me the invisible things is all livin' up my gall bladder—but he's goin' to be kind enough to cut open my body and take it out for me. Well, I'm not fool enough to sign my own death certificate, thank you very much. *(Crossing down front.)*

What do I do? I get up out of the bed, which is the only furniture in the room, and I'm lookin' at him the whole time—starin' him right in his little piggy eye, the bloody bastard—and I take my time walkin' to the bathroom, just like I was in my own house... And then I slam the door hard enough to be heard in hell! Twice more the little bastard tried to get me to give him my gall bladder. Bastard. No good talkin' to the people who brought me food. They were all workin' for him. Thought he was a bleedin' genius with his ideas about little invisible animals crawlin' around makin' people sick. So then they move me to another hospital—out on North Brother Island. Right in the middle of the East River, off 138th Street. They called it an "isolation center." I spent three years in that place. Three years never gettin' to be with anybody. Them just bringin' my meals to the door and shovin' them in, and then runnin' away like I was some kind of leper. Me, never sick a day in my life—except for the fever on the crossin'—and that was just bein' in steerage. *(She crosses back to the potatoes and picks one up thoughtfully.)*

They let me out four years ago. Somebody must have gotten tired of Soper and his stories. Or maybe Soper gave up on havin' my gall bladder. But of course, they had to do it up official, like they hadn't kidnapped me. I'm supposed to be reportin' to them on my "activities" every three months. *(She laughs.)* Made me sign a paper that I'd never cook for a livin' again. Now that was charitable of them, don't you think? Maybe they was hopin' I'd hire on as the president of a bank. *(She laughs again.)* They fix it so there's only two ways a woman can get by, don't you know. Them Sopers of the world. *(She hacks a potato.)*

I'm a cook. I made good money, too. Of course, I was goin' back to it. But then I find out that Soper's been to the agencies. The little bastard went to Stricker's and Seeley's and took 'em my picture, and told them all about my gall bladder. Can you believe it? The only two agencies in New York, and so now I can't get on. Bastard. *(She chops potatoes.)*

Death. Them rich folks will spend a pot of money lookin' for it. Makin' up fairy stories, huntin' down innocent people. They go trackin' down death like it was some kind of mystery. Didn't a million people starve to death in Ireland while the rest of the world stood around biddin' over the bones? Didn't my own mother die the death of a dog on that ship while the rich folks looked down over their railin's at us like we were just so many animals in a filthy cage? And where is the city in the world that doesn't have a street for the buyin' of a girl's body and the sellin' of her soul? You don't need a microscope to see death. *(She holds up a potato.)* It's as big and as plain as a potato. *(She laughs.)*

But I'll tell you a secret. They'll never come lookin' for me here— the Sloan Hospital. Dr. George Soper and his cronies wouldn't be caught dead in this place! *(She whispers.)* Do you know why? It's a public maternity hospital. *(She throws back her head and shouts.)* There's nobody here but poor women and their starvin' babies! *(She laughs uproariously. The lights fade to the sound of her laughter.)*

**BLACKOUT**

**END OF PLAY**

# "The Potato Song"

## (Traditional Melody)

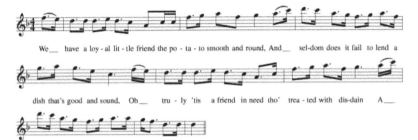

We__ have a loy - al lit - tle friend the po - ta - to smooth and round, And__ sel-dom does it fail to lend a

dish that's good and sound. Oh__ tru - ly 'tis a friend in need tho' trea - ted with dis-dain A__

most es-sen-tial food in-deed that ful-ly earns its fame.

# THE PARMACHENE BELLE

**SYNOPSIS:**

The play opens on the day that "Fly Rod" Crosby is scheduled for knee surgery. "Fly Rod" is a six-foot-tall, masculine woman who works as a Maine hunting guide at the turn of the century.

She is concerned about leaving the hospital in time to rendez-vous in New York with Annie Oakley at the annual Sportsman's Exhibition. Aware of Annie's traumatic history of abuse as a child, "Fly Rod" has become obsessed with "rescuing" her.

"Fly Rod's" fantasizing is disrupted when she opens the gift that Annie has sent her. She is shocked to discover it is the arrow case that belonged to Annie's friend, the martyred Indian warrior, Sitting Bull.

This play is a meditation on outsiders and survivors, people who have become separated from their tribe. It is a play about coming into the world with blasted prospects and hopeless odds, and negotiating that exceedingly fine line between denial and faith, self-delusion and affirmation, radical vision and insanity.

1 woman
35 minutes
Single set

# CAST OF CHARACTERS

CORNELIA "FLY ROD" CROSBY: A tall, 42-year-old
    woman of masculine appearance.

SCENE: A hospital room in the Eye and Ear Hospital, Portland,
Maine.

TIME: January 1899.

# THE PARMACHENE BELLE

*A hospital room in the Eye and Ear Hospital, Portland, Maine, January 1899. There is a bed with several pillows piled against the headboard, and a small table with a bouquet of flowers, some books, and a collection of photographs of Annie Oakley. There is also a photograph of a group of outdoorsmen. A brown package tied with twine is at the foot of the table.*

*A split-bamboo fly rod leans against the bed. CORNELIA "FLY ROD" CROSBY, a tall woman with masculine appearance, 42, enters using a cane. Dressed in period long johns with a much-worn fly-fishing vest, she wears a battered felt hat, with hand-tied flies in the hatband. She is suffering from an excruciating knee injury and makes her way painfully to the bed. She seats herself gingerly on the edge of the mattress, easing the injured leg onto it. Once in position on the bed, she picks up the fly rod as a distraction.*

FLY ROD: *(After a moment, she reels in.)* Not hittin' too good today, are they? Ayuh. Let's see what we got on here... *(She examines the leader.)* Ayuh. Got a brown hackle on the end of the tippet and a dragonfly on the dropper. Well, that tells the story plain enough... Imitations. Got nothin' but imitation flies on here. *(Looking up.)* Know what an imitation is, don't you? Somethin' that's tryin' to look like somethin' that it's not. Now, let's see... *(She takes her hat off and examines the flies on the band. After a moment, she selects one.)* I think this is what the doctor ordered. *(She holds it up.)* The Parmachene *[pronounced "par-ma-chee'-nee"]* Belle. Ayuh. The Parmachene Belle... *(She begins to remove the brown hackle.)*

I've been a Maine huntin' guide for almost twenty years, and there aren't many flies I haven't seen. Royal Coachman, Professor, Scarlet Ibis, Grizzly King, Queen of the Waters... I've used 'em all... But if I had to do with just one fly, it would be the Parmachene Belle. Caught two hundred trout in one day at Kennebago with this little beauty. *(Holding up the Parmachene Belle.)*

95

our third year, and it's goin' to be the finest ever. *(Picking up the rod.)*

I asked her to meet me there, because I've got something' pretty special to tell her. I've been thinkin' about it all winter, laid up here with this rimracked knee. I would have written it to her, but it didn't seem like the sort of thing for piecin' out a letter—pastin' it in somewhere between "how's the weather" and "yours truly." Besides, that business manager of hers—Frank Butler—he reads all her mail. Ayuh. I gotta be outta here in six weeks. And I've gotta be walkin'. *(Suddenly jerking the rod.)* See that! Thought we had a strike. *(She laughs and sets the rod on the bed.)*

So me and this Boston pen-pusher we're out on Cupsuptic in my bark—my canoe. It's late in the afternoon, about four o'clock, and the water's so calm it looks like a sheet of glass. We've been out about two hours without so much as a rise, when suddenly the water starts dimplin' up in front of us. Trout comin' up to feed. And pretty soon the water is just boilin'with 'em. So the sport starts castin', and I don't mind tellin' you that little pen-pusher could lay one of the prettiest casts I've ever seen—right over the boil, and do it again and again. But—nothin'. Whatever he was sellin', those trout weren't in the mood to buy. So he starts fumdiddlin' with his flybook, lookin' to "match the hatch," as they say. Might as well have been sortin' sawdust. By now, those trout were gettin' tired of waitin' on him, and they were startin' to sink... so I take out my rod. Well, pen-pusher fellow sees this and he gets himself all humped up like a hog goin' to war: Just what kind of fly do I think is goin' to do a better job than his hand-tied, custom-deluxe, fish-scale, cork-body, wiggle-waggle imitations? So I show him the Parma Belle—just like this one here. *(Picking up the rod.)* Well, that bit of red feather was like a matador's cape to a bull. He takes one look at it and he's *off.* *(She imitates him.)* "What's *that* supposed to be?" And I say, "A Parmachene Belle." And he says, "But what's it *supposed* to be?" And I look at him, calm as a clock, and I say, "A Parmachene Belle." *(Setting down the rod.)*

Well, his face is lookin' like a starched shirt. He's come all the way down from Boston with a flybook full of imitations of every creature that ever crawled or hatched its way off of Noah's Ark, and here's this jillpoke of a huntin' guide from East Overshoe—a *lady* guide at that—and he's payin' her his good money to go fishin' with a fly that doesn't look like anything God ever put on this earth. And if that's not enough to make Napoleon cry, it's a fly with a red feather! Well, that Boston lawyer, he just starts plasterin' it all over the wall, about folks from the State of Maine in general, and about ladies from the State of Maine in particular—and he's tellin' me how it's just like a woman to be gettin' all notional about the fancies—pickin' out her flies the way she would be pickin' out a hat.

Tell you the truth, I don't remember too much of what he said after that, because it was just about then a twelve-inch lunker smashed the Parma Belle clear to the gills, and after that, I had my hands full just keepin' her on the line. Well, the pen-pusher durn near tips over the bark, grabbin' for his rod, and he's starts whippin' the water some fierce. Meanwhile, I'm pullin' 'em out of the water, one right after the other—sometimes two on the line! By the time the sun went down, I had me the prettiest gad of trout you ever laid your eyes on. *(Shaking her head.)*

Boston fellow never got a single strike. Skunked. Ayuh. And he was singin' pretty small on the way back to camp, but I told him not to feel too bad about it, because the trout that took the Parma Belle were probably just the females anyway... out shoppin' for hats when they should have had their mind on feedin.' *(She laughs and picks up the rod.)*

I guess you could say I'm a bit of a Parmachene Belle myself. Six feet tall and a huntin' guide. Not too many other gals like me. *(She pauses thoughtfully.)* None, in fact. But I get the strikes. Ayuh. Everything hits the Parma Belle. Of course, you don't want to keep everything that hits—just the ones that are sportin'. That's why, when the men come girlin', I always toss 'em back. The men will hit anything. *(Pausing thoughfully.)* Too much like landin' chub. *(She laughs and then becomes serious.)* Women—they're the keepers. *(She jerks the line.)* See that! Had a hit there! *(Laughing abruptly, she drops the rod and sits back on the bed.)*

Knew I was a fancy as early as I can remember. Knew there wasn't goin' to be any husband and there weren't goin' to be any babies for me. My pa died when I was two, and my brother and I had to learn to paddle our own canoe pretty young. So did Missie. That's one of the reasons we get on so well. She's a fancy, too, only she doesn't know it yet. Or maybe she does, but she's been bein' Annie Oakley for so long, she doesn't know what to do about it.

Well—I knew I was goin' to need a man's job to pay for myself and my mother. Women's jobs don't pay enough to live on, because they figure on a woman havin' a husband—or havin' to get one. So I took my inheritance—every penny of it—and spent it on the fanciest girls' boardin' school in the State of Maine. Ayuh. That's just what I did. And I don't regret it a whit. It was two of the best years of my life, livin' up there in Augusta with all those girls. Oh, we had some wild times...

But, after graduation, they all went on to Vassar and Smith and Wellesley, and I went back to Farmington. One of the girls' daddies had gotten me a job in his bank—clerkin'. It was a man's job and I told myself I was lucky to have it. And I was... I didn't have to get a husband. But it just seemed like life was goin' on everywhere else, and I was missin' it, humped over that desk and stackin' up numbers from sunup to sundown. I started coughin', and then I started losin' weight, and my head was hurtin' all the time. The doctor told me if I didn't quit my job and start spendin' more time out-of-doors, I was goin' to die. *(Pausing.)*

There comes a time when the thing that's keepin' you alive starts to be the thing that's killin' you. Ayuh. That's what's happenin' to Missie now.

So I quit the bank, and I moved out to Rangeley to take a job housekeepin' at one of the fancy resort hotels. It was women's work, and I didn't how long I could stick it, but at least, when my chores were done, my time was my own. I got to know the huntin' guides who were always around, and they started teachin' me to fish and to shoot. And then Charlie Wheeler sent me a five-ounce, split-bamboo rod—one of the first fly rods he ever built. I'll never forget what he told me. Charlie said, "Here—take it! And if it doesn't work, break it up and throw it away and forget I ever made such a crazy thing." *(She laughs.)* I've been earnin' my livin' with that "crazy thing" ever since.

It was different for Missie. With Missie, it was always guns. Ayuh. Always guns. *(She pauses.) Her* pa died when she was six, but she already had five sisters and a baby brother. She was out trappin' birds for the family to eat by the time she was seven, and then, when she was eight, they sent her to earn her keep at the county poor house. And that's where the trouble started. But she doesn't want anyone to know about that.

Missie's a private person, and she's got good reason to be. That's why bein' Annie Oakley is so hard on her. But Frank Butler, he just can't see it. And why should he? *She's* the laborin' oar in that dory. You know, he's her manager. He's not really her husband. Not really. Oh, I'm sure it's all legal *now*, or the papers would have got hold of it. She couldn't be travelin' around with an unmarried man—or a married one—he was married before, you know—not if she cared about her reputation, and that is one thing about Missie: She cares about her reputation. Oh, she *cares* about her reputation. I'd guess that's about the most important thing in the world to her, and that's because of what they did to her. Ayuh. That's the key to the whole thing.

So she got herself a husband, because how was it goin' to look for a single woman to be pitchin' her tent with a camp full of five hundred cowboys, Indians, and roughriders? Now, it was just the opposite for me. If I'd had a husband, it would have been the ruin of my reputation. What kind of man was goin' to go off in the woods with another man's wife?

I understand Missie. I know what she needs. That's because we're both fancies. I knew it right when I first met her, three years ago. It was my second year with the Sportsmen's Exhibition. In fact, the whole Maine exhibit had been my idea in the first place. We'd had such a success the first year, all kinds of folks were wantin' to climb aboard. There were manufacturin' folks all over the country shippin' us flyfishin' rods and rifles, and the Spaldin' Brothers, who just opened themselves a fancy new store over on 42nd Street—they sent me a custom-made, designed-in-Paris, green suede ladies' huntin' outfit. And that's what I was wearin' the first time Missie saw me. That green huntin' outfit was the talk of Madison Square Gardens, let me tell you! There wasn't a single reporter who covered the Exhibition who didn't have somethin' to say about my skirt bein' seven inches off the floor. Ayuh. My ankles got more press than the sixteen-pound salmon, the wild cat, *and* the baby moose!

But it was that green suit that attracted Missie to me. And that's when I knew she was a fancy. Most of the women who saw me sittin' there in front of Camp Rangeley with my rifle and my short skirt, they were too scared to come over and talk to me. Afraid it might be catchin', I guess—but Missie, she walked right up and started askin' if she could look to see how it was made. She sews all her own costumes, and that short skirt was real interestin' to her, because she has to jump over tables, turn somersaults, and ride a bicycle in her act. What with her concern about her reputation, you can see why this was a problem for her. She told me what she does is sew elastic on the inside hem of the skirt and then attach it to her boots. That's what holds her skirt down. She was real excited to see that folks like the Spaldin' Brothers were openin' up a line of clothing for sportswomen.

She gave a talk last year at the Exhibition: "Sports for Women." Should have called it "Guns for Women." That's really what she talked about—how women should feel as comfortable holdin' a rifle in their arms as they would a baby! She was teachin' 'em what kind of gun to keep beside the bed at night, and how to hide a pistol down inside their umbrellas when they're out walkin'. Made some of the menfolk a little edgy, but the women were real attentive. There's some folks who criticize Missie because she's not out workin' for the Suffrage vote, but the way she tells it, what the women of this country need is not ballots—but bullets! *(Laughing.)*

But I know this—if I'd been wearin' that Spaldin' Brothers suit back in September when I stepped off that train, you wouldn't see me laid up in this hospital now. I was wearin' a regular ladies' skirt, with a heavy, old hem draggin' after me like an anchor. I jumped off the train before it had come to a dead stop, but that hem had got

102

itself caught, and next thing I knew, I was bein' hauled down the tracks, my knee all sideways to Sunday. *(Pausing.)*

The doctors are sayin' I'll never walk again. *(Changing the subject abruptly.)* Missie sent me a get-well present. Want to see it? *(Pause.)* Well, *do* you? *(She waits for an affirmative and then crosses to retrieve the parcel.)* So do I. I've been savin' it. Thought I'd open it right before they come to take me for the surgery. Give me somethin' happy to think about. *(She shakes it.)* Well, it's not a gun. Not heavy enough. *(She sets it within reach by the bed.)*

I'm not takin' any chances with the surgery today. No, sir. I'm not takin' any chances on missin' that Sportsman's Show. I asked one of the nuns here what she does when she's got a patient all fetched up on a dead-end road, and she told me she prays to Saint Anthony. He's the patron saint of lost causes.

Now I'm a pretty hard-headed gal when it comes to believin' in miracles. Like I said, I've been paddlin' my own canoe for a long time. But the way I see it, prayin' is sort of like flyfishin'. Maybe the Great Spirit, or God, or whatever's gonna take the hook, and maybe not, and maybe prayin's about as foolish as spittin' on the bait—but there's some master smart anglers been known to spit on the bait when no one was lookin'!

So I've made a sort of a deal with Saint Anthony. I promised him that, if could walk again, I would raise the money to build a chapel up there in Oquossoc, and I'd dedicate it to Our Lady of the Lakes. Now, if that's not chum-choppin' the bait and spreadin' it on the water, I don't know what is. *(Smiling.)* Missie would say it was a crate of hogwash. *(Pausing.)* Maybe so. *(She becomes serious.)* But I'll tell you somethin'—this "Annie Oakley" business is goin' to kill her, if she keeps on the way she's goin'.

She's thirty-eight. Missie's gettin' tired. She can't keep goin' the way she did when she was twenty. And now Bill Cody's got the Wild West Show back on the road, doin' a hundred and fifty stands a season—two shows a day. Missie told me she was havin' to go out in that arena in blizzards with the wind howlin' around her, and they were makin' her shoot when the rain was comin' down so hard she couldn't look up to see the traps. Told me she had to wear a leather skirt and rubber boots, with the mud up to her knees sometimes—and comin' home to a tent! Eatin' out of a mess hall, too, with five hundred other folks, most of them men.

Don't get me wrong—nothin' the matter with workin' with men. I do it, too, when the season's on—but in the winter I come home to the women. Ayuh. Always come home to the women. I got me a little house over to Phillips, and the ladies and me, we organized ourselves into a sort of a club called the King's Daughters. Every Monday night, the women come over, and we practice our music, or read poetry or stories out loud to each other, or catch up on our sewin'. And there's the New England Women's Press Club. I like to have them over for what I call my "pink teas." Took forty of the gals on a trip through Rangeley last summer. There—*(Indicating a bouquet of flowers.)* See that? Those are from the Press Club. *(She rises and begins to cross to the flowers.)*

But what does Frank Butler think about bein' back on the road? He eats it up. *(Taking out a flower from the Press Club bouquet.)* I should press this and send it to Missie. *(She takes out one of her books.)* Ayuh. That Frank Butler's a real handshaker. Looks good, but that's about it. *(Arranging the flower between the pages of the book.)* Missie loves flowers. Puts 'em around the outside of her tent when she can. *(Closing the book and leaning her weight on it.)* Nothin' Mr. Butler likes better than goin' smilin' with the boys, dressed up like a deacon and talkin' big—tellin' stretchers about himself and Missie. *(She opens the book to look at her work.)* She hates it. I never met a woman in my life who set more store by honesty, and here she's got this fellow tied to her saddle when every other word out of his mouth is a little north of north. *(Taking out another flower.)* Maybe I'll send her two. *(She arranges the flower for pressing.)*

Ayuh. The tourin' life suits a handshaker like Frank Butler. It's killin' Missie, but he'd be the last to notice, with her pullin' in six hundred dollars a month—which is more than folks in Maine make in a year—not countin' the fact he doesn't have to pay for his food or his tent! And what does he do for his share? He calls himself her "business manager," but how much business can there be to manage when Missie's been with the Wild West Show for fifteen years? *(She slams a stack of books over the one she's using to press flowers.)* He's her *husband. (She slams the books again.)* That's what he's paid for. *(Pausing.)* She's payin' him for bein' her husband. *(Another slam.)* If you're thinkin' I'm fixin' on taking Missie away from Frank Butler, that's *exactly* what I'm goin' to do. And I'm not apologizin' for it, either, because the way she's livin' now is killin' her.

*(Crossing back to the bed.)* You know there' a lot of folks can't be around Missie. They say she's "particular." And she is. She's got to have everything in just the right place, and she can't stand a speck of dirt. Takes a bath three times a day, too. Ayuh. You just try puttin' somethin' back wrong and she'll give you the very jessie! I know... I've heard her do it! And she's got every minute of the day planned out, too. What time to get up, what time to eat breakfast—same exact breakfast every day—and how long to read the paper, how many rounds of powder she's goin' to fire. She's got everything all planned out to a tee.

A lot of folks won't have anything to do with her, and truth be known, she's just as happy to have it that way. But they're wrong when they think it's Missie. It's this "Annie Oakley" business that's makin' her that way. It's her havin' to move all the time, havin' to be somebody she's not.

What Missie needs is a place in the country, away from people. A quiet place where she can rest and sew and read—or just look out the window if that's what she wants to do. She's earned it. And if she wants to work a little, she can do that, too. The sports in Rangeley would pay good money to say they'd shot with Annie Oakley. She could be a huntin' guide if she wanted. And, in the winter, she can come stay with me in Phillips. I've got plenty of room. *(Picking up the rod with increasing agitation.)* What she really needs is fly-fishin'. Ayuh. Fly-fishin's just the thing when a body's wound up tighter'n a fly reel. That's Missie. *(Angry and frustrated, she aims the rod like a rifle and pretends to shoot it.)*

Pull! BANG! Pull! BANG! Pull! BANG! Or, sometimes, when she throws five eggs in the air—BANG-BANG-BANG-BANG-BANG!

Just point that gun, BANG, and it's done. Well, fly-fishin's not like that at all. You have to wait. A lot of waitin'. *(Sighing, she sits back.)*

And you can't be splashin' around while you wait, either. You have to make yourself part of the river. I think that's the hardest thing for the sports—bein' part of the river... Fishin' downstream, watchin' where your shadow is, keepin' your voice low... and waitin'. *(Pausing.)* Some folks just don't know how to wait. But you can't be in a hurry when you're fly-fishin'. *(She takes a deep breath. Closing her eyes, she begins to put herself into a trance.)*

Sometimes I like to slip the bark out on the lake before the sun's up, when it's still dark. Be out in the middle of Mooselemeguntic before the camps are up. So quiet... just the sound of the paddle, dippin' so soft, it sounds like a dog lappin' water. *(She opens her eyes.)* Everything so still, like the seventh day of creation... Finished... perfect... And then the mist starts to scale off a little bit, and the sky starts to get lighter—just enough to make out the shape of the tackle in the bottom of the canoe. And then you hear it...the first birdsong!

And then a breeze comes up and starts rifflin' the water a little bit. And all the time, when you weren't noticin', it's been gettin' lighter and lighter—so now you can see the silhouette of the trees on the edge of the lake, and some of the camps, and then—there it is! — that big, red-orange ball, risin' over the Height of the Land... *(She opens her eyes.)* That's when you realize it doesn't make a damn bit of never-mind if you catch a fish or if you don't, because it's somethin' just to have lived in an hour like this. *(Pausing.)*

Missie was raped when she was nine. *(Pausing)* Not just once. Over and over. For two years. She was hired out to a family. She calls them "the wolves." They starved her and they froze her and they beat her. And all the time, the he-wolf was rapin' her. She was afraid to run away, because she thought they were sendin' money home to her brothers and sisters. Turns out they weren't even doin' that. *(Shaking her head.)*

Guns and money. That's Missie's religion. And target practice... that's her prayers. Ayuh. Livin' short... I don't care how much they pay her. That is livin' short. *(Pausing to check a watch in one of her pockets.)*

Well, almost time for the sawbones to cut. I better open up my good-luck charm. I'm bettin' it's a quilt, or maybe a piece of fancywork. Missie's always sewin' on somethin'.' *(She picks up the package and begins to open it. It's not necessary for the audience to see what is in the box. FLY ROD is startled by the gift. She looks at it for a long time before she speaks.)* I know what this is. She showed it to me last year in Boston. It's an arrow case. *(She closes the lid of the box slowly.)* It's Sittin' Bull's arrow case that he had with him at Little Big Horn, when he took Custer's scalp. Sittin' Bull... only Missie calls him somethin' else—"Tatanka..." *(Pausing to remember and giving up.)* Somethin'... his Indian name. *(Setting it down, visibly upset.)* I can't believe she sent this to me. I thought it would be a piece of fancy work—somethin' she made with a needle. *(After a moment, she picks it up again.)*

They shot Sittin' Bull about five years ago. Missie won't talk about it. He was family to her, and Missie doesn't have family... Why would she send me his arrow case? *(She sets it aside again.)* Maybe she doesn't want to remember. *(She pauses.)* He was Ghost Dancin.' He was Ghost Dancin' and they told him not to, but he was doin' it anyway. Ghost Dancin' to bring back the buffalo and make the white man disappear. They say when some of them dance long enough, they get themselves into a trance where they believe they're in that world already.

Missie wouldn't have had any patience with that. She wanted Sittin' Bull to come back to the Wild West Show, where he was safe and where he could make a lot of money. But he wanted to dance the Ghost Dance with his people... So they shot him. *(She looks up.)*

They say, when they shot him, his horse started bowin' and kneelin'—doin' tricks like it was back at the Wild West Show. *(Pausing.)* That was Ghost Dancin', too, I guess. *(She picks up the box again.)*

107

Why would she want to send me his arrow case? *(After a long pause.)* Maybe… it's because she knows I'll be huntin' again, after the surgery. *(With increasing energy.)* Because Sittin' Bull was a hunter… and so am I! I'll bet that's it. *(Relieved, she sets the box on the floor by the bed.)* Well, I'm just goin' to have to ask her when I see her in New York. Ayuh. I'm just goin' to have to do that! *(Looking up.)*

So—I guess, it's time for me to be reelin' in. *(Smiling.)* Now, you remember what I told you… *Everything* hits the Parmachene Belle. *(She begins to reel in. Blackout.)*

**BLACKOUT**

**END OF PLAY**

# HARRIET TUBMAN VISITS A THERAPIST

**SYNOPSIS:**

*Harriet Tubman Visits A Therapist* is a gripping confrontation between two women who share the same oppression, but whose definitions of survival are in direct conflict.

Harriet Tubman, suspected of planning an escape on the Underground Railroad, has been sent to the Therapist for an evaluation. The Therapist, another African American captive, warns Harriet about the dangers of radical action. Harriet accuses the Therapist of colluding with the enemy in the guise of practicing therapeutic intervention.

As the Therapist attempts to convince Harriet of the benefits of accepting the things she cannot change and learning to live one day at a time, Harriet uncovers the Therapist's secret—a secret which will give her access to the information she needs.

The plot takes a sudden twist during one of Harriet's spells of sleeping sickness, and in resisting the suggestions which justify the Therapist's ideology, Harriet discovers a source of spiritual support rooted in her own activism.

Two women
20 minutes
Single set

## CAST OF CHARACTERS

HARRIET TUBMAN:  An African American woman, mid-twenties.

THERAPIST: An African American woman.

.

**SCENE:** Interior of a therapist's office.

**TIME:** Another dimension of space-time.

*"She declares that before her escape from slavery, she used to dream of flying over fields and towns, and rivers and mountains, looking down upon them 'like a bird,' and reaching at last a great fence or sometimes a river, over which she would try to fly, 'but it 'peared like I wouldn't hab de strength, and jes as I was sinkin' down, dere would be ladies all drest in white ober dere, and dey would put out dere arms and pull me 'cross.'"*

—From an article about Harriet Tubman
in *The Boston Commonwealth*, 1863.

# HARRIET TUBMAN VISITS A THERAPIST

*A contemporary therapist's office with pictures of peaceful landscapes and recovery literature in the bookcase. There is a desk, but the THERAPIST has done much to create a non-threatening, informal atmosphere. The THERAPIST is reviewing HARRIET's file. She is a light-skinned African American woman who wears the clothing of a contemporary middle-class therapist. There is a soft knock on the door. The THERAPIST closes the file and rises*

THERAPIST: Come in. *(There is another knock, and she crosses to the door and opens it. HARRIET TUBMAN stands in the doorway. HARRIET is a dark-skinned African American woman, about 27, wearing the clothing of an enslaved field worker. HARRIET's speech and movements are deliberately slow and dull at first. She stands waiting for orders, head bowed.)*Come in. Harriet Tubman? You're right on time. *(She gestures into the room. HARRIET lifts her eyes briefly. Her face is expressionless.)* Please... Either chair. Make yourself comfortable. *(HARRIET shuffles towards one of the chairs and sits. She keeps her head down. The THERAPIST sits in her chair. There is a long silence. The THERAPIST sighs and smiles at HARRIET.)* I understand that you have spells of narcolepsy... *(No response.)* You have brief periodic spells of deep sleep? *(HARRIET nods briefly, eyes down.)* And they can come on any time—when you're working? *(HARRIET nods again.)* Ever since you were a girl, wasn't it? *(HARRIET glances at her quickly, then down again.)* I understand that's when these spells came on— when you were a girl...

HARRIET: Dey come on when de man thow'd de chunk o' lead in mah face.

THERAPIST: And you were a girl then?

HARRIET: Not aftuh dat.

THERAPIST: How do you feel about that? *(HARRIET lowers her eyes again.)* I would feel pretty angry if someone threw a lead

113

weight at me. *(HARRIET remains motionless. The THERAPIST changes her tone.)* Harriet, do you know why you're here?

HARRIET: Massuh Edward done sent me.

THERAPIST: Do you know why?

HARRIET: Cain't sell no nigga like me.

THERAPIST: I don't think that's why. *(HARRIET looks down.)* I understand why you feel that way. That's a very natural conclusion for a slave to draw. But in this case, I think Mr. Brodas is genuinely concerned about you, and I have reasons for why I say that. Do you want to hear them? *(No response.)* I think Mr. Brodas likes you. He speaks about you with a great deal of pride. He's allowed you to choose your own husband, and John Tubman is a free man. That's a very unusual thing for a slaveowner to do. And he lets you hire out to a shipbuilder—

HARRIET: He take alluh money.

THERAPIST: Well, that's not exactly true. I understand that you get to keep what you make over what you owe him. *(HARRIET snorts.)* I understand you've been able to buy yourself a pair of oxen. That's pretty impressive. *(No response.)* You could even buy your freedom someday.

HARRIET: Time I'ze daid.

THERAPIST: *(The THERAPIST studies HARRIET for a moment.)* You know I share your feelings about slavery. All day long I listen to women tell me stories that make me sick. Stories of rape—raping children, of beating—beating pregnant women, stories of murder, or torture, of live burnings, of babies being sold away from their mothers, of chain gangs... *(HARRIET looks away.)* But I'm not going to change it, and neither are you. We can drive ourselves crazy thinking about it. We can kill ourselves fighting it. Or we can make the most of what is possible. Like you did, buying your oxen.

HARRIET: *(Eyes down.)* Nat Turner.

THERAPIST: What?

HARRIET: *(Looking at the THERAPIST for the first time as she speaks, HARRIET drops the dull-witted act.)*
Nat Turner. He kill fifty-seven whitefolks.

THERAPIST: *(Taken aback by HARRIET's intensity.)* They hanged Nat Turner.

HARRIET: *(Looking at her hands, acting again.)* Hanged a man las' week over to Bucktown for stealin' chickens.

THERAPIST: *(Losing her temper.)* Nat Turner is the reason you can't read. Did you know that? After his uprising, they made it illegal to teach slaves to read or write. After Nat Turner, we couldn't even meet to go to church, unless a white man was the preacher. After Nat Turner, they wouldn't let us talk to each other in the fields, but they wouldn't let us just work either. Oh, no. After Nat Turner, we all had to sing while we worked—oh, except of course, "Go Down, Moses." Now, thanks to Nat Turner, you can die for singing that song.

HARRIET: *(Singing.)*
O GO DOWN, MOSES,
WAY DOWN IN EGYPT'S LAND...

THERAPIST: You think I'm an uncle tom, don't you?

HARRIET: *(Continues singing.)*
TELL OLE PHARAOH,
LET MY PEOPLE GO...

THERAPIST: You think I sold out.

HARRIET: *(Closing her eyes, she raises her voice.)*
OLE PHARAOH SAID HE WOULD GO CROSS,
O GO DOWN , MOSES,
LET MY PEOPLE GO,
AND DON'T GET LOST IN THE WILDERNESS,
LET MY PEOPLE GO.

*(HARRIET looks at the THERAPIST, who is silent now.)* Didn't hab no gun.

THERAPIST: Who didn't have a gun?

HARRIET: Prophet Turner. A sword. Can you see dat? Had hissef a sword! What he gonna do wid a sword? Slit open de sow's belly? *(She laughs.)*

THERAPIST: Are you thinking of killing someone?

HARRIET: *(Looking at her hands.)* Mebbe I buy a mule to go 'long wid de ox.

THERAPIST: *(Sizing her up.)* I'm going to be frank with you. Mr. Brodas has sent you to me, because he's afraid you're going to run away.

HARRIET: *(Bursts out laughing.)* Oh, he skeered!

THERAPIST: *(Pleasantly.)* Well, that's why you're here, and I'm afraid I have to agree with his observation.

HARRIET: *(Enjoying the idea.)* He tell you dat Harriet bin lookin' mighty greazy. *(She laughs.)*

THERAPIST: "Greazy?"

HARRIET: Gonna to slip hersef th'oo de massuh's han's. *(She laughs again.)*

THERAPIST: *(Smiling along with the joke.)* Your husband seems to think you've been "lookin' mighty greazy," too.

HARRIET: *(She stops laughing.)* John say dat? He tell you dat?

THERAPIST: He told Mr. Brodas. *(HARRIET is stunned.)* Harriet, nobody's against you here. Your husband loves you and Mr. Brodas has a great deal of respect for you. But, if you run away, neither one of them is going to be able to save you from the slave catchers—or

116

their dogs. You've got too much to live for to throw your life away like that.

HARRIET: John bin talkin' to Massuh Edward?

THERAPIST: (Rising.) Harriet, I want to help you. You are in a very serious situation. Mr. Brodas has asked me to determine whether or not I think you're going to run. *(HARRIET looks at her.)* I'm going to tell him that I'd like to see you for a few more visits, but after that, unless there's a change in your attitude, I will have to tell him the truth. I doubt he'll let you hire out after that. *(HARRIET says nothing. The THERAPIST turns suddenly.)* Look at you! You're young, you're healthy, you're in love, you work for wages, your husband is a free man—That's a lot to be thankful for! You have less reason to run than most. *(HARRIET remains silent.)* And what about your family—your mother? She was the one who saved your life when you got the head injury, wasn't she? She was right there with you, wasn't she? Are you going to abandon her? You know you'll never see her again. *(HARRIET looks down.)* And what about John? He's a good man, Harriet. You're pushing away the people who love you in the name of freedom. You're so busy dreaming about a world you don't have, you're missing out on the one right here. Learn to focus on the things you *can* change, learn to appreciate what you have right now—and you can be a great force for good. Little by little, one day at a time, you life will get better and better. *(HARRIET says nothing. The THERAPIST sits at her desk and looks out the window.)* I knew a woman once who decided to run. You could say she'd been "lookin' mighty greazy." One night, she took her two daughters—one was six and the other twelve—and she ran. *(HARRIET is keenly interested. The THERAPIST turns back to her.)* They caught her, of course, as they catch most runaways.

HARRIET: How far she git?

THERAPIST: To the Delaware border. *(HARRIET nods. The THERAPIST narrates the rest of her story with clinical detachment.)* It was the hounds that got her. By the time they called off the dogs, her daughter—the six-year old—was already dead. And then they took turns raping the twelve-year old while they

117

made the mother watch. After that, she wouldn't have anything to do with the child. She wouldn't touch her, wouldn't talk to her. She treated her like she didn't exist. Right up until the girl was sold down South. *(HARRIET says nothing.)* Do you think this woman made a wise decision?

HARRIET: She didn't hab no gun?

THERAPIST: What if she had? She was outnumbered. Or do you think she should have shot her daughters?

HARRIET: (Shrugging.) Lib in de no'th or die in de south.

THERAPIST: You would shoot your own children?

HARRIET: I seen mah sistuhs—Linah and Soph— seen 'em sol' off on the de chain gang, an' dat day I wisht dey wuz daid, an' I bin prayin' dey was daid ev'y day aftuh dat, too.

THERAPIST: Enough to kill them?

HARRIET: Ain't no livin' when dey kin do yo' body any way dey like.

THERAPIST: *(Vehement.)* Oh, yes, there is! We are so much more than our physical bodies—

HARRIET: *(Cutting her off, she rises.)* Look! Now, you look! *(She pulls her shirt out and pulls up the back.)* Heah—you look at dat. You look at what de white man done.

THERAPIST: (Turning away) I've seen plenty of scars.

HARRIET: No, you look, cuz you ain't seen dis 'oman's scars. You therapizin' on me, you look. You stan' up heah, an' you look. *(The THERAPIST looks.)* You see dat? Dat is a fiel' o' flesh been ploughed by de debil's own han.'

THERAPIST: But you *don't* have to let it scar your soul.

HARRIET: What you talkin' 'bout? Mah soul? Dis heah is mah soul! Dis black Ashanti skin is mah soul! *(She turns to face the THERAPIST.)*

THERAPIST: *(Becoming very clinical.)* And what does it do for you to keep remembering?

HARRIET: *(HARRIET starts to respond with anger, but she stops herself. A smile spreads slowly over her face.)* You is sleepin' wid de massuh.

THERAPIST: *(Hesitating, she chooses her words carefully.)* Sometimes Mr. Brodas visits with me. *(HARRIET is still smiling.)* That doesn't affect my belief that your running away would be suicidal.

HARRIET: (Lowering her head.) Yas'm.

THERAPIST: And it doesn't affect the fact I want to help you.

HARRIET: (Mumbling.) No'm.

THERAPIST: You don't have to put on an act for me. *(HARRIET looks up, puzzled.)* I know what you're doing. *(Silence.)* You don't have to please me.

HARRIET: *(Eager to please.)* If you doan' want me to be pleasin,' den I won't. No ma'am. Sartainly I won't. You des see how unpleasin' Harriet kin be. I kin be de downright unpleasin'est—

THERAPIST: *(Cutting her off.)* Stop it!

HARRIET: Yas'm. *(The two women sit in silence.)*

THERAPIST: (Starting over.) I sleep with Mr. Brodas... *(Hesitating.)* He's a kind man.

HARRIET: Oh, yas'm, dat he is. He be de bes' massuh in de world! Dat's des what I allus say, dat Massuh Edward, he—

THERAPIST: *(Cutting her off.)* I hate him. *(HARRIET watches her.)* I hate him, because he's white, because he's a slaveowner, because he's a drunkard, because he's a coward and a liar, I hate him because he uses women, I hate him because he doesn't bother to wash when he comes to me. I hate him so much, believe it or not, he doesn't bother me. I hate him so much, I don't let him have anything.

HARRIET: He got yo' body.

THERAPIST: I'm not in it. *(HARRIET says nothing.)* I haven't been in it since I was twelve and I watched the dogs tear my little sister to pieces. I had already left my body before the first white man climbed on top of me. And I wasn't in my body when they raped my mother. I wasn't in my body when they sold me down south. And I wasn't in my body when I had a white man's baby at thirteen. I wasn't in my body when they sold her five years later. And I wasn't in my body when Mr. Brodas made his proposition. But, you show me your skin, Harriet—let me show you my soul. It's here... *(She takes out a locket.)* This is my daughter, Felicity. She lives with me. She has never had to work in the fields, and she never will, because I am buying her freedom. This, this is my soul. I keep myself alive for her.

HARRIET: While you is larnin' de other women to be de slaves.

THERAPIST: I teach them how to survive. Look—these are my files. Here are the stories of women who've come to me. Women who didn't go crazy, who didn't kill themselves. Women I *helped*. And I have helped women, Harriet. Maybe not you. But I have helped women. *(She pauses. HARRIET says nothing.)* I give them a safe place to express themselves—to let out their grief and their rage. I help them speak the unspeakable. I listen. I validate their suffering. I teach them strategies for surviving— *(She breaks off.)* You think this is bullshit. *(HARRIET says nothing.)* How many women could live day to day with your level of rage? You don't have children. What do you think that anger would do to a child? And how long do you think *you're* going to be able to live like this? Oh, you can make a run for it, all right. But Pennsylvania is a long way off. Do you really think you're going to have the stamina to make it? It takes a cool head to go the distance, and I can tell you right now, Harriet Tubman, you don't have it. Your rage will get you over the county line, maybe. But the Delaware border? Unh-unh. Never.

HARRIET: *(The THERAPIST has hit a nerve, and HARRIET reconsiders.)* So when you work wid de women...

THERAPIST: I teach stress management... relaxation techniques. Visualization. Sometimes I do a guided meditation with women.

HARRIET: An' dat is what?

THERAPIST: That is where I put the client under hypnosis—which is like your sleeping spells—and then I talk them through an experience they're afraid of—like a whipping, or an auction where their children are going to be sold... or I prepare them if they have to submit sexually to their owner. *(She pauses.)* I give them images—I teach them to go away... so they can bear it.

HARRIET: An' dis keep de women goin'?

THERAPIST: Yes. Yes, it does. They learn that reality is only another state of consciousness, and it gives them some control. Otherwise, of course, they have none.

HARRIET: *(Making up her mind.)* You bin up no'th.

THERAPIST: I was captured.

HARRIET: You bin to Delaware.

THERAPIST: To the border.

HARRIET: Draw me dat map.

THERAPIST: I can't do that. *(HARRIET looks at her.)* I don't encourage my clients to take reckless chances with their lives.

HARRIET: *(Angry, she rises.)* I got two rights—de right to freedom and de right to die.

THERAPIST: *(The THERAPIST rises.)* I have the right to live.

HARRIET: Libbin'! What you talkin', 'oman? You ain't eben inside yo' own skin! *(HARRIET, enraged, turns to go. She opens the door, but is seized by a fit of narcolepsy. The THERAPIST helps her to a chair. She watches HARRIET for a moment, and then she closes the door.)*

THERAPIST: You want the map? All right, Harriet Tubman, I'll give you the map... Oh, I'll give you the map. *(She pulls a chair close to the "sleeping" HARRIET.)* Harriet, listen to me. We don't have very much time, and I want you to listen and remember. You are standing in the middle of a field. It's the field behind the Brodas plantation. It's night time, Harriet, and you are alone. You are standing in the field, and you are looking back towards the cabins. Can you see them? *(HARRIET doesn't move.)* It's dark, and everyone is asleep, Harriet, everyone except you. You are wide awake, standing in the field. You turn back towards the cabins—and there's your cabin—can you see it? Nod your head if you can see it. *(HARRIET still doesn't move, and the THERAPIST discovers the cause of her resistance.)* Harriet, listen to me. You are having to go alone. You are leaving tonight. John is asleep in the cabin. You are leaving without him. Can you see the cabin where John Tubman is sleeping? *(Slowly, HARRIET nods.)* It's a clear night and the stars are out. Look up, and see if you can see one star that's brighter than the others, the one in the "drinking gourd." It should be right over the cabins. Do you see it? *(HARRIET nods.)* Good. That's the North Star. You're going to keep that in front of this shoulder. *(She taps HARRIET's left shoulder.)* This shoulder. Now remember that. It's a warm night, Harriet, and you're not afraid. Lift up your arms. Lift them up. *(HARRIET lifts her arms slightly.)* Are you ready? *(HARRIET nods.)* Take a deep breath, and as you breathe in, feel yourself becoming lighter. Breath in again. You are becoming lighter and lighter, lighter than a feather. Lighter than the smoke of a candle flame. Keep breathing in. You are rising in the warm air. Feel yourself rising. Your toes are just barely touching the ground... just barely, and now they're not touching at all. You are rising like smoke, up over the field. Higher and higher. Look down, Harriet, and see the cabins. They're just little boxes under you, as you rise higher and higher, keeping that North Star over this shoulder. *(She touches her again.)* And now you're over the big house... You're flying over the edge of the fields now, over Greenbrier Swamp. You can see the black water shining through the trees with the reflection of the moon. And you stay on the edge of the swamp, Harriet. Can you see it? *(She nods.)* And now the swamp is opening up, widening. And you're over the Choptank River. The Choptank River is right under you. And you're flying faster now, because you need to keep going, over the Choptank, and it's getting smaller and smaller. Follow the Choptank, Harriet, about seventy miles on the Choptank River. And see where you are now? See the river, how small it is? It's just a stream now, isn't it? *(HARRIET nods.)* You're very close to the Delaware border now. Very close. There's a farm on the other side of the border, the Cowgill farm in Willow Grove, and that's all you need to know, because once you get to the Cowgill farm, they'll take care of you the rest of the way into Pennsylvania. All you have to do is get to the farm. You understand? *(HARRIET nods.)* So you're going to go down now. Down through the trees, down into Delaware. You're almost on the ground now, almost touching the ground... Listen! Listen, Harriet! Hear that?  What is it? Listen! *(HARRIET stiffens.)* It's dogs barking, isn't it? Hear them? It's the dogs, Harriet! The dogs! They're after you. You can hear them coming. And you start to run, Harriet. *(HARRIET's breathing accelerates.)* Run! Run! And you're running, but it's night, and you can't see very well. You're tripping over the tree roots and the branches, and the dogs are getting louder and louder. *(HARRIET begins to breathe heavily.)* And now you can hear the men shouting! Listen! They've fired a shot! They hear the dogs, Harriet, and they're after you, and there's nowhere to hide. They're coming. And you're running so fast you can't breath, and your heart is pounding so hard in your chest it hurts. And now you turn around, and you can see them, Harriet. You can see the dogs coming for you. And you know what they're going to do. You've seen them catching possums and squirrels. And you know what they're going to do to you. And you're trying to run, but you trip. You're on the ground, Harriet, and you can't get up. And now, I'm going to count backwards from five—

HARRIET: *(Breaking through with great effort, but still in a trance.)* I see dem! I see dem!

THERAPIST: You see the dogs?

HARRIET: I see de women.

THERAPIST: What women?

HARRIET: De women wid de lights. I see dem in de trees aroun' me. I see dem stretchin' out dey han's to me. Dey is callin' my name, an' I am reachin' out my han's to dem.

THERAPIST: There aren't any women with you. You are alone.

HARRIET: No, dat I ain't. I has got de company of so many women, dat I cain't see dem stars no mo' for de brightness of de women dat is 'roun me in dem trees. And dey is callin' out my name, say "Araminta"—dat what dey callin' me—"Araminta"—like my mamma. Dey is shinin' wid glory, dese black women, an' dey is reachin' out dey han's to me, gonna pull me up off of dat groun,' gonna snatch me right 'way fum de mouf dem dogs and de han's of de white man. Gonna pull me on ober dat line. Doan matter I cain't walk, doan' matter I cain't run, doan matter I forget de way—doan matter, 'cuz dese women, dey been heah befo' and dey gonna bring me on acrost. Dey is shinin' an' laughin' an' dey is takin' me by de han' to freedom.

THERAPIST: Are you dying, Harriet?

HARRIET: *(Laughing in her trance.)* No, ma'am! Not befo' I live to see de lights of Phil'delphia!

THERAPIST: Harriet, these women don't exist.

HARRIET: Oh, yes, dey do. Dese is de women dat lib so good dey cain't die. Dese is de women fum Africa, de women who pitch deysefs off de ship, rather die dan lib in de chains ob slavery. Dese is de women who kilt dey own chilrun 'fo' dey see dem sol' on de auction block… de women who kilt dey massuhs wid de ax, wid de

124

hoe, wid dey bare han's, de women dey cain't skeer no mo' cause dey already done do de wors' an' dey still alibe. Dese is de women larnin' each other de ways to keep out de white man's babies befo' dey start growin' in de womb ob de black woman's body... de women wid de spells make de whitefolks sick. Dese is de African women, de Ashanti women.

THERAPIST: *(Quietly.)* I can't see those women. *(Smiling in her trance, HARRIET begins to sing, and the THERAPIST talks over her singing.)*

| HARRIET | THERAPIST |
|---|---|
| O GO DOWN MOSES, WAY DOWN IN EGYPT's LAND... TELL OLE PHAROAH LET MY PEOPLE GO. | Harriet, I'm going to count backwards from five. And when I say "one," you will open your eyes. You will be relaxed and fully alert. You will not remember any of this experience. Five... four... three... two... *one.* |

*(HARRIET opens her eyes, and the two women look at each other. The THERAPIST smiles.)*

THERAPIST: How do you feel?

HARRIET: *(After a long pause.)* You sic de dogs on me.

THERAPIST: *(Pretending not to understand.)* I'm sorry?

HARRIET: You sic de dogs on me. De white man's dogs.

THERAPIST: I don't know what you're talking about.

HARRIET: De dogs in yo' haid. You ain't buyin' no freedom fo' nobody wid dem dogs in yo' haid.

THERAPIST: *(Opening HARRIET's file.)* Harriet, I am going to have to recommend to Mr. Brodas that you be removed from your present position and put in the fields to work where there is closer supervision.

HARRIET: Put me in de prison—I'ze gone. All de chains in de worl' cain't keep me now. My freedom ain't in the de han's of you or Massuh Edward or eben in mah own han's. *(The THERAPIST is busy writing. HARRIET crosses to the door, and looks back.)* Mebbe I come back. When I do, mebbe I take your daughter. *(She exits, leaving the Therapist standing.)*

**BLACKOUT**

**END OF PLAY**

# ARTEMISIA AND HILDEGARD

**SYNOPSIS:**

*Artemisia and Hildegard* features two of the most famous women artists in history, together on an explosive arts panel about survival strategies for women artists.

Hildegard Von Bingen, German abbess from the 12th century, and Artemisia Gentileschi, Italian baroque painter from the 17th century, have been scheduled as guest speakers on a panel titled, "Women Artists: Strategies for Survival." As the women display slides of their work, the sparks begin to fly. Confronted with conflicting philosophies, each woman attempts to seize control of the panel.

The debate takes a personal turn when the women are compelled to reveal secrets of their childhood, secrets which have shaped their mutually-exclusive strategies for survival. Contradictions and compromises are revealed, and the panel ends on a dramatic high note, when the audience is recruited to take sides in the debate.

Two women
One hour
Single set

# CAST OF CHARACTERS

ARTEMISIA GENTILESCHI:  A woman in her fifties, masculine in appearance.

HILDEGARD VON BINGEN:  A woman in her fifties.

**SCENE:** A stage set for a conference panel at the actual theatre, university, or event where the play is being presented.

**TIME:** The present.

# THE PAINTINGS

1) Untitled illustration from *Scivias*, Hildegard von Bingen. ("Nun receiving inspiration")

2) Untitled illustration from *Scivias*, Hildegard von Bingen. ("Ring of flames with flower center")

3 *Judith Slaying Holofernes*, 1612-13, Naples, Artemisia Gentileschi.

4) *Susanna and the Elders*, 1610, Artemisia Gentileschi.

5) *Lucretia*, 1621, Genoa, Artemisia Gentileschi.

6) *Judith Slaying Holofernes*, 1620, Florence, Artemisia Gentileschi.

# ARTEMISIA AND HILDEGARD

*A stage set for a conference panel. Upstage right, there is a large screen on which the images of the paitings will be projected. (The paintings provide a significant dramatic element, and care should be taken to display them prominently.) There is a podium centered to the left of the screen, and on either side are two chairs of identical make. Next to the podium is a small table with a full water pitcher and two empty glasses. There is a sign on the podium that reads, "Women Artists: Strategies for Survival."*

*ARTEMISIA GENTILESCHI enters and seats herself in the chair to the left of the podium. ARTEMISIA is a woman in her fifties of masculine appearance. She is dressed expensively, but conservatively in a tailored men's business suit. Making no contact with the audience, she rises to pour herself a glass of water, sits down again, and begins to look over her notes.*

*After a moment, HILDEGARD VON BINGEN enters. She is also a woman in her fifties. She wears a feminine, flowing robe or dress suggestive of a priestess in a contemporary goddess cult. She is carrying a bouquet of flowers along with her notes.*

*HILDEGARD freezes when she sees ARTEMISIA. ARTEMISIA, absorbed in her notes, does not notice her. HILDEGARD sweeps to the podium and bangs her folder down on it. ARTEMISIA turns to look at her, but HILDEGARD pretends not to notice, addressing her remarks to no one in particular.*

HILDEGARD: I knew there wouldn't be any flowers. Why is it whenever they have a panel on art, there's never the slightest attempt to be decorative? I've gotten so used to it, I just bring my own anymore... Now do you see anything I can put these in?

ARTEMISIA: *(Rising.)* Hildegard von Bingen?

HILDEGARD: *(Pretending to see her for the first time.)* Oh… Yes? That's me.

ARTEMISIA: I'm Artemisia Gentileschi. I met you last year at the conference for the National Museum of Women in the Arts. *(Extending her hand.)* We were on the panel about "Images of Empowerment."

HILDEGARD: (Looking past her to the pitcher.) Oh… Here! You don't mind, do you? *(ARTEMISIA withdraws her hand. HILDEGARD places the flowers in the pitcher and proceeds to arrange them.)* They really should have given each of us a pitcher. What did they think, we would be passing the water back and forth? There. That looks a little more artistic, don't you think? *(ARTEMISIA is starting back to her seat, when HILDEGARD turns to address her.)* Well, yes. Last year in Washington. Yes. "Images of Empowerment." That was certainly a free-for-all, wasn't it? I'm not sure I would have agreed to be on the panel if I'd known that the moderator would be so unable to keep order. Not very empowering, if you ask me—a group of women shouting at each other… I wonder where the other artists are?

ARTEMISIA: There aren't any others.

HILDEGARD: Oh, really? Well… that's a surprise. They told me it was going to be a panel. You can hardly call two speakers a panel, can you? It's more like a debate, wouldn't you say? And I'm not at all sure I came here to debate.

ARTEMISIA: I'm just going to show my work and then answer questions… *(She sits.)*… if anybody has any.

HILDEGARD: Yes. Well, I just wish they had told me ahead of time. *(She sits.)* Somebody apparently saw to it that you had the information.

ARTEMISIA: Well, I asked.

HILDEGARD: *(Ignoring the remark, she looks at her watch.)* I wonder where the moderator is… It's past time to start.

ARTEMISIA: There isn't going to be a moderator.

HILDEGARD: No moderator. No decoration for the podium. No other panelists. Well... I really don't like having to introduce myself.

ARTEMISIA: Do you want me to do it?

HILDEGARD: Oh... well... I...

ARTEMISIA: Is there anything particular you want me to say?

HILDEGARD: No, just tell them who I am... *(An afterthought.)* You can leave out the part about my sainthood. It tends to put audiences off. *(ARTEMISIA crosses to the podium.)* No, I tell you what. Why don't I introduce you first, and then you can introduce me?

ARTEMISIA: I don't care. *(HILDEGARD sweeps to the podium, as ARTEMISIA returns to her seat)*

HILDEGARD: Good evening, ladies and gentlemen. I am Hildegard von Bingen and on behalf of [name of sponsoring theatre, organization, college, etc.] I would like to welcome you to our panel tonight, "Women Artists: Strategies for Survival." It is my privilege to introduce the other speaker tonight, my distinguished colleague Artemisia Gentileschi. *(Turning to ARTEMISIA with a smile.)* Artemisia is a painter from the 17th century, Italy, isn't that right? *(ARTEMISIA smiles, and HILDEGARD turns to the audience.)* At a time when few women were allowed a career in the arts, she was fortunate enough to have been born the daughter of Orazio Gentileschi, one of the most successful painters in Rome. *(ARTEMISIA is disturbed by this reference. She grows increasingly uneasy during HILDEGARD's introduction.)* He not only encouraged his daughter's interest in painting, but he taught her as if she were his apprentice, a role usually reserved for males. It was through his interest and support that she gained the *patronage* of some of the most influential *men* in Italy—Michelangelo's great nephew and the members of the Medici family, I believe—patronage which virtually *guaranteed* the success of her work.

Many of her paintings have been mistakenly attributed to *male* painters of her day, and it is only just now that historians and art critics are beginning to recognize these paintings as the work of a *female* artist… a task which has been difficult because her work so closely *imitates* the styles and the themes of the men with whom she competed—*(ARTEMISIA rises abruptly and crosses to the podium, cutting off HILDEGARD.)*

ARTEMISIA: Thank you, Hildegard.

HILDEGARD: Oh, but I wasn't through.

ARTEMISIA: That's all right. I really just like to let the art speak for itself.

HILDEGARD: Well, but you can't separate the artist's experience in life from her art.

ARTEMISIA: I can.

HILDEGARD: But I'm sure you'll agree that one of the ways in which the work of women artists differs from the work of men—

ARTEMISIA: *(Interrupting her.)* I don't identify myself as a woman artist. Gender has nothing to do with my art. I'm a painter, who just happens to be a woman.

HIILDEGARD: *(Addressing the audience with mock innocence.)* Well… I don't know what to say. I guess I just expected that for a panel titled "Women Artists," they would have invited guests who identified themselves as "women artists—"

ARTEMISIA: *(Cutting her off.)* Do you want me to introduce you?

HILDEGARD: If you like… Certainly. *(She returns to her seat, flush with victory.)*

ARTEMISIA: It's my pleasure to introduce the other member of the panel tonight, my distinguished colleague, Hildegard von Bingen.

*(HILDEGARD smiles at the audience.)* Hildegard von Bingen is a nun—

HILDEGARD: *(Interrupting.)* Abbess.

ARTEMISIA: ... *abbess* from the 12th century, Germany. Hildegard is a woman of many accomplishments... *(She nods to HILDEGARD, who acknowledges the compliment.)* ... so many, in fact, I don't know if it's possible to focus on any one of them and still do her justice. *(HILDEGARD begins to grow uneasy.)* Hildegard writes religious skits for the nuns to perform for each other, and she has also written some religious songs—

HILDEGARD: (Interrupting.) I prefer to use the word "spiritual" instead of "religious," and they are polyphonic choral works.

ARTEMISIA: Ah. And she has also written a *spiritual* book—

HILDEGARD: *(Interrupting.)* Three.

ARTEMISIA: *Three* books which describe in detail her *spiritual* visions—

HILDEGARD: *(Interrupting.)* Mystical visions.

ARTEMISIA: Would you like to take over?

HILDEGARD: *(Smiling broadly.)* No, you're doing just fine.

ARTEMISIA: She has also written several self-help books on herbs and nutrition. And between writing all these books, she has somehow found time to design the illustrations for them, although the actual painting of these is done by the nuns who share her commitment to *collective* art and *anonymity*...

HILDEGARD: *(Cutting in.)* That's not entirely accurate.

ARTEMISIA: Did I leave something out?

HILDEGARD: No, dear, what you said was fine. *(She rises and crosses to the podium.)* Thank you. *(ARTEMISIA sits, and HILDEGARD addresses the audience.)* I appreciate Ms. Gentileschi's introduction, but I am afraid that it might have created an unfortunate impression about the nature of my art. *(She turns to ARTEMISIA.)* And, Artemisia, I certainly don't want you to feel that this is a criticism of anything you said. *(To the audience.)* It's just that secular artists have difficulty grasping the experience of the spiritually-minded artist. It requires another model to comprehend the work of the mystic—another dimension of thought, if you will. Now I'm going to ask you to take a little mental excursion with me for a moment, to leave the auditorium and enter into the world of your imagination. We are going to travel to a little village in Germany together, and we are going to visit a child who lives there. Not your usual curious toddler, with her chubby little arms and legs so busy, busy, busy. No, we are going to visit a very different little child. She lies very still on her bed, as quiet as a mouse, not moving at all—but she's not asleep. Far from it! Her tiny eyes are wide open, as she watches a bright ring of light, like a halo, fill her room. And she is listening to voices that no one else can hear. Her little brain is seared with constant pain. This is a very different child, not at all like her nine brothers and sisters, and her parents know this, and they love her all the more for being so special—but... they don't know what to do with her! They are tormented with her anguish, and they ask God constantly what is his will for this little one. And the answer they receive, breaks their heart: Give her back to God. What parent could bear to part with their own child— especially one so helpless and so vulnerable? But this child's parents were as special as she was. They were willing to put obedience to God ahead of their own selfish pleasure. And so, when their daughter was only eight years old, they took her to a Benedictine monastery, where she could grow up in God's house— far from the distractions and cares of most girls her age. *(ARTEMISIA shifts her notes. HILDEGARD, picqued by the distraction, crosses in front of the podium to address the audience.)* How many of you know what an anchoress is? *(She looks for a show of hands.)* That's too bad, because it has been an important tradition for a select number of women. An anchoress is a woman who has chosen to give herself to God, much like a nun, except that the anchoress chooses to cut herself off even from the world of the convent. She chooses to spend her entire life inside her cell, dedicating herself to the life of the spirit. Her initiation rite is a funeral service, symbolizing the fact that from this time on, for all intents and purposes, she is dead to the world. After the ceremony, she enters her cell, and the entrance is walled up... except, of course, for an opening for food and so forth. *(Pausing.)* Obviously becoming an anchoress is a radical step for a woman to take. It is a path of extreme devotion to God. When I was eight years old, my parents, in the supreme sacrifice of their lives, took that radical step for me. I was sealed up inside a cell with another anchoress, a woman named Jutta, who had been a friend of our family. I did not set foot outside that cell for ten years. *(Crossing back up to the podium, she notices the look of shock on ARTEMISIA's face.)* You're wondering why I go into this. Because, unlike our friend Artemisia, I cannot separate my life from my art. My art is a revelation of the spirit which I cultivated for all those years in the confines of that cell, learning to discipline the will and dedicate myself to God. It is impossible for you to understand my art without understanding my life, and it is impossible for you to understand my life without my art. This panel is titled "Women Artists: Strategies for Survival." This is the survival strategy I have come to share with you. My art has been preserved for *eight* centuries... *(She points this to ARTEMISIA.)*... not just two. And that is because it is part of not just my life, but the life of an entire community of women. We share in the creation of each other's art, and because of that, the art belongs to all of us. It becomes a vital part of our history and our tradition, and that is why my songs and my books and my paintings have been cherished and preserved for eight hundred years. They have been passed on by the *women* for whom they were created. *(ARTEMISIA turns toward her to say something, but HILDEGARD cuts her off.)* Perhaps this would be a good time to show the first slide. *(The first slide comes up, a picture of a nun dictating to a scribe. HILDEGARD views it with obvious satisfaction.)* This is an illumination from my first visionary work, *Scivias*, or "Know the Ways of the Lord."

ARTEMISIA: Is this a self-portrait?

HILDEGARD: *(Smiling.)* Let's just say it's a portrait of a nun who is receiving her inspiration to write directly from God, which is how

I wrote *Scivias*. You see, nuns were not allowed to learn reading or writing.

ARTEMISIA: But you did.

HILDEGARD: *(Leaning across the podium to address ARTEMISIA.)* Well, here is the remarkable thing—I learned them without having to learn them. *(Turning back to the audience.)* At the age of forty-two, I received this vision of blinding light, which felt like it was permeating every cell of my brain, and after this vision, I found that I not only knew how to read and write in Latin, but that I intuitively understood the meaning of all the chapters in both the Old and New Testaments!

ARTEMISIA: *(Openly skeptical.)* Without reading them?

HILDEGARD: *(A patronizing smile.)* How could I? It was forbidden. *(ARTEMISIA shakes her head in disbelief, and HILDEGARD crosses quickly in front of the podium to upstage her.)* And this vision was accompanied by a voice, a voice that said, "O fragile one, ash of ash and corruption of corruption, say and write what you see and hear!" And this vision was repeated three times. Well, of course, I had such a low opinion of myself, and so much doubt because of what the monks had taught us about ourselves... *(She points this last remark toward ARTEMISIA.)*... well, naturally I ignored the voice, feeling that it couldn't really apply to me. And of course, I was punished for this, as we always are for ignoring the will of God. I became deathly ill. I lay in my bed completely unable to move. *(Crossing back to the podium.)* The Abbot of Kuno came to see me in this condition, and I couldn't even turn my head to look at him when he entered my bedchamber—not even when he ordered me to! And this act of insubordination from a woman filled him with holy terror. He realized I must have been responding to some authority higher than his own, and like most men, he could not imagine what that could be unless it was God. Needless to say, the Pope responded immediately with permission for me to write whenever I felt called to do so. And that is what this illustration symbolizes. The special dispensation of knowledge to women, not learned from men, but received *directly* from Spirit.

138

ARTEMISIA: With the Pope's permission.

HILDEGARD: The point I am making is that women do not have to be dependent on men for our language or our arts. *(To ARTEMISIA.)* Do you know, I invented my own language? I designed an alternative alphabet. I didn't even use the same letters as the men. And I only taught it to women. The point is, women have our own unique relationship to God, and we need our own language, our own iconography, our own techniques for expressing this. *And* we need communities of women. Of course, this is incomprehensible to women who think like men, women who produce their work for purely commercial purposes. Money is an invention of men, and to get their money, you will, of course, have to do what they want you to. And that is the prostitution of a woman's art and of a woman's soul. *(ARTEMISIA starts to say something.)* But I was talking about the special language of women. Could we see the next slide, please? *(The slide of the ring of flames comes up, with its obvious reference to the vulva. HILDEGARD turns conspiratorially toward the audience.)* Here is another illumination from the *Scivias*.

ARTEMISIA: *(Sarcastically.)* What is it?

HILDEGARD: *(Smiling at ARTEMISIA.)* A painting in the secret language of women. *(Turning back to the slide, she recites with overt eroticism:)*

*Oh tender flower of the meadow*
*and O sweet sap of the apple*
*and O harvest without pith*
*which does not divert hearts to sin.*
*O noble vessel which is not defiled*
*or consumed in the dance*
*of the ancient cave, and which is not oozing*
*with wounds of the ancient destroyer.*

*(Addressing the audience.)* I wrote that poem for Rupertsberg. *(To ARTEMISIA.)* You cannot understand my art, unless you understand Rupertsberg. *(To the audience.)* Rupertsberg was a glorious experiment. Rupertsberg was my greatest trial and my greatest achievement. Every woman needs a Rupertsberg. And every woman

could have a Rupertsberg if she would only learn to fight for it, as I did. Rupertsberg was my convent. *(Crossing in front of the podium.)* You remember that my spiritual life began as an anchoress at a monastery, where I shared a cell with another woman named Jutta. Over the years, Jutta and I began to acquire a reputation for our spirituality, and a number of women were attracted to our lifestyle as anchoresses. *(She smiles at the audience.)* The monks had to expand our little cell over and over again to accommodate the new arrivals. We found, after a decade, we had become a convent. Jutta was the head of it until she died, and then I was elected prioress, at the age of thirty-eight. Shortly after that, I received the greatest vision of my entire life. *(Pausing for effect.)* I had a vision to take the women away from the men. *(She laughs.)* Well, you can imagine how popular that was. The monks were in a complete uproar. They were, of course, thinking about what men always think about: money. You see, the young women who came to the monastery would bring their property with them, which would contribute to the wealth of the monastery. And then, of course, there were gifts from their rich relatives. And, to be perfectly honest, I was, by now, the chief spiritual and material asset of the monastery. The goose that laid the golden egg, so to speak. *(She laughs.)* No, they did not want to see me leave and take the nuns with me. And, of course, some of the parents of our girls were in a tizzy about the move. You see, the monastery had all the comforts of home: Great stone buildings, acres and acres of cultivated fields, and a very celebrated vineyard. Rupertsberg, fifteen miles down the river, had nothing but a few temporary buildings. It was a desert by comparison. Everyone asked me, "What is the point of moving the sisters from a place where they are perfectly comfortable to such great poverty?" The point? We would be away from the men. What greater poverty is there, than for women to live in the shadow of men? Of course, that's not what I told them. *(She returns to the podium.)* I argued that the austerity of the conditions would force us to rely more on the grace of God… *(Turning with a smile toward the image.)* And on each other.

ARTEMISIA: But you still needed the men's permission to move.

HILDEGARD: *(Turning to ARTEMISIA.)* Of course. But the point is, we got it.

ARTEMISIA: Like asking your husband for a night out with the girls.

HILDEGARD: *(Icy.)* We were not wives.

ARTEMISIA: What's the difference? You couldn't own anything, you couldn't read or write, you couldn't go anywhere—

HILDEGARD: *(Cutting her off.)* The difference is we didn't have to sleep with them. *(Crossing in front of the podium to address the audience.)* Yes, we had to work around the men. Every woman has to do that. But the question is, does she work around them for her own gain at the expense of other women—or does she work around them to help liberate her sisters? And there is nothing more tragic than a woman who can't tell the difference. Let me tell you a story. A story of a nun. Her name was Richardis, and I loved this girl as I have loved no other. She was my joy in living. She was my right hand. I taught Richardis everything I had received from revelation. She was by my side the entire time I was writing *Scivias*. In fact, she took down the dictation for much of it. I would have walked through fire for Richardis, and I believed she would have done the same for me... but I was wrong. *(Crossing back behind the podium.)* After we moved to Rupertsberg, she began to change. She became cold and unfriendly. You see, her affection for me had been based on my status among the monks. When I removed myself and my nuns from the monastery, she began to treat me with contempt. Richardis simply could not see the world except through the lens of male approval.

ARTEMISIA: What happened to her?

HILDEGARD: Oh, she began to use her family connections to get herself appointed abbess at another convent—one connected with a monastery. I knew this would be her destruction. I warned her, but she wouldn't listen. You see, I had lost my credibility with her when I chose to separate myself from the men. She saw me as a woman who had dropped out of the race, when the truth was I had set my sights on a prize higher than anything men could bestow on me.

ARTEMISIA: Did she get the appointment?

HILDEGARD: It was not the will of God for her to have it. I did everything I could to block it. I even went so far as to ask the Pope to intervene.

ARTEMISIA: *(This sabotage hits a nerve with ARTEMISIA.)* You were jealous of her.

HILDEGARD: *(Defensive.)* Me? Richardis was the jealous one! She just couldn't wait to prove her teacher wrong. I could see her whole plan—she was setting herself up to become a rival abbess. She was only twenty-eight, but she wanted to prove to me that she could get her appointment ten years sooner than I had gotten mine. She was going to take my best nuns with her. Her convent would have all the material comforts we left behind when we founded Rupertsberg. Oh, she was going to show me! And the saddest thing was, she really believed the men were on her side. They were just using her as a pawn to get to me. Do you know what they did the day she left Rupertsberg? They sent an emissary to come get her, in case I tried to use physical force to restrain her. Can you imagine the humiliation? Rescuing the girl from my evil clutches! It was quite a show, let me tell you. I learned a very painful lesson that day about putting my trust in human relationships instead of divine love.

ARTEMISIA: So she did get the appointment after all.

HILDEGARD: *(Studying ARTEMISIA.)* Yes, she did get the appointment, but she was only able to keep it for a few months.

ARTEMISIA: You had her transferred.

HILDEGARD: No. *(Smiling to herself.)*No, Richardis died.

ARTEMISIA: *(Angry.)* You don't sound very sorry.

HILDEGARD: I was sorry when her soul died, but I had already grieved that death. The death of her body did not interest me. *(ARTEMISIA turns away in disgust, and HILDEGARD responds with aggression.)* But how can I expect you to understand the agony of spiritual motherhood? What could you know about the passage of a soul from carnal desire to spiritual joy—a passage a hundred times more dangerous and difficult than the contractions of a physical labor? What would—

ARTEMISIA: *(Cutting her off abruptly.)* Do you have some more slides?

HILDEGARD: *(Brought up short by ARTEMISIA's commanding tone, HILDEGARD breaks off.)* No, I've taken enough time. *(To the audience.)* Thank you. You've been a wonderful audience of women. *(She collects her notes, crosses to her chair, and sits.)*

ARTEMISIA: *(She rises, crosses to the podium, and takes a moment to arrange her notes.)* Well... *(She smiles at HILDEGARD.)* Hildegard is a tough act to follow. *(Turning back toward the audience.)* I'm just going to show some paintings and tell you a little about them. I don't really have any fancy philosophy. My formula for survival is pretty simple: Make it great. Great art is around for a long time, and nobody forgets the woman who made it, even if they do get the name mixed up from time to time. *(She smiles at HILDEGARD, who ignores her.)* I know Hildegard and her nuns find poverty uplifting for the soul, and maybe it's because I'm not religious—or,"spiritual—" *(Another smile in HILDEGARD's direction. ARTEMISIA crosses in front of the podium.)* But poverty has not been good for my soul... or any other part of my anatomy. Poverty makes me hungry and nervous, and I don't paint well when I'm hungry and nervous. Poverty makes me buy cheap materials, and I don't like to work with cheap pigment. And poverty makes a girl get married when she doesn't want to. My daughter is never going to have to do that, because she is never going to be poor. May we see the first slide please? *(This is the Naples version of Judith Slaying Holofernes. She allows the audience a moment to look at the work before she speaks.)* This is the first painting I did after I left home. It's called *Judith Slaying Holofernes*. I was nineteen. Hildegard should recognize the subject.

HILDEGARD: Oh, yes.

ARTEMISIA: *(Crossing to the slide.)* Judith was an Israelite. She was a widow. That's her in the blue dress. And she had a companion named Abra. That's Abra in the red. Anyway, Judith and Abra's village was being attacked. They were under a siege, running out of food. So Judith and Abra went to pay a visit to the enemy general. Judith pretended to like him, and she and Abra got him falling-down drunk, and then they cut off his head. Which, even if the man is passed out, is pretty hard to do. I mean, he's going to have a certain number of reflexes—and then, of course, there's the technical problem of the cervical vertebrae, which overlap each other. You'd have to actually cut through the bone... *(HILDEGARD clears her throat. ARTEMISIA smiles at her.)* I was concerned with the emotional realism of the subject. Most of the painters who did Judith showed her standing at arm's length, holding out the sword like this... *(She illustrates.)*... looking squeamish. Well, you can't even slice a ham from that position, much less the neck of a two-hundred-and-fifty-pound man. I wanted to get across the idea that Judith was an ordinary woman, who would encounter the same problems as any one of us, if we were to cut off a man's head.

HILDEGARD: Did you bring some other slides?

ARTEMISIA: *(To the audience.)* We'll come back to this later. Next slide, please. *(Susanna and the Elders comes up on the screen.)* This is *Susanna and the Elders*.

HILDEGARD: *(Needling ARTEMISIA.)*Ahh... You painted that during your trial, didn't you?

ARTEMISIA: *(Ignoring the reference to her past.)*I painted it when I was sixteen.

HILDEGARD: But wasn't it related to your courtroom experience...?

ARTEMISIA: *(Cutting her off abruptly.)* My art is not related to my experience. Didn't I say that earlier? *(Turning to the audience.)* The story of Susanna, like the story of Judith, is from the Bible. Well, not actually from the Bible, but from the Apocrypha. *(To HILDEGARD.)* As the resident abbess, would you like to tell us about the Apocrypha?

HILDEGARD: No, go ahead. It's your painting.

ARTEMISIA: Basically the Aprocrypha is the part of the Bible, where they moved all the deviant women. It's not considered to be the word of God like the rest of the Bible, which is why the women like Susanna and Judith were moved there—away from the important males in the Bible. Kind of like Rupertsberg.

HILDEGARD: *(To the audience.)* We moved ourselves to Rupertsberg.

ARTEMISIA: Yes, of course. But the point is, many people will never know the stories of Judith and Susanna, because they have been *separated* from the mainstream Bible stories. *(Before HILDEGARD can respond.)* Are you familiar with Esther's remark in the Apocrypha?

HILDEGARD: Which one?

ARTEMISIA: The one where she doesn't want to marry the king, and she says she'd rather wear a menstrual rag on her head than a crown?

HILDEGARD: Do you have a painting of that?

ARTEMISIA: Would you like to commission one?

HILDEGARD: I could never justify the expense.

ARTEMISIA: I was talking about Susanna. *(Turning back to the painting.)* She's taking a bath, and these men are spying on her. They're elders of the church. They've just thought of this plan where they tell Susanna she has to let them rape her, or else they're going to make up a story that they caught her having sex with someone other than her husband, which, since women weren't allowed to testify, would mean an automatic death penalty. *(To the audience.)* Susanna is a popular subject for painters, voyeurs, and rapists. Rembrandt, Tintoretto, Rubens—they've all tried to do her. They usually show her trying to protect her body. Since the men are asking her permission to rape her, I don't think that's very realistic. Susanna can refuse. In fact, she does. When the woman is covering herself like this, or like this... *(She demonstrates the poses.)*... she

145

is relating to her body the same way the men are. Susanna doesn't do that. If she saw her body as an object to protect, she would probably have said yes, because letting them rape her was supposedly going to save her life. But she said no, which means she did not see the body as a thing apart from herself.

HILDEGARD: Excuse me, Artemisia?

ARTEMESIA: Yes?

HILDEGARD: Don't you think that her refusal might have had something to do with her principles?

ARTEMISIA: *(Angry.)* No I don't. The men are disgusting. They are so repulsive, she doesn't even relate their threat to her sexuality, because it's obvious that these men could never in a million years even come near it. She relates to them as if they were a pair of mayflies, buzzing around her head. That's what I was trying to convey with the pose.

HILDEGARD: *(Baiting ARTEMISIA.)* Susanna went to court, didn't she?

ARTEMISIA: *(Angry.)* It wasn't her idea.

HILDEGARD: But they *did* find her innocent.

ARTEMISIA: *(Abruptly.)* She should never have been accused. Next slide. *(The slide of the Genovese Lucretia comes up.)* This is Lucretia. It's hard to see the detail on the slide. It's so dark. But she has a knife in her left hand, and she's holding her breast with her right. *(She looks at the slide.)* I don't know if you can see this, but she's holding her breast like this… *(She demonstrates on herself.)*… pushing it up, and then squeezing the nipple out between the second and third fingers—like she's getting ready to nurse. Lucretia was a Roman woman. She was raped by her brother-in-law, and she killed herself so that no one could accuse her of having cheated on her husband.

HILDEGARD: Why is she holding her breast like a nursing mother if she's going to stab herself?

ARTEMISIA: Why do you think?

HILDEGARD: I don't know. That's why I asked.

ARTEMISIA: *(To the audience.)* I wanted to illustrate that she is torn between the demands of her motherhood—to stay alive for the sake of her children, and the demands of her husband—to kill herself in order to save his honor... That's the whole problem with Lucretia. Her body belongs to her husband and her children. It's not even hers. That's why she kills herself. *(To HILDEGARD.)*She identifies herself as a woman.

HILDEGARD: She needs a spiritual sense of herself.

ARTEMISIA: She needs a career.

HILDEGARD: *(Smiling.)* Then she would just belong to the career instead of a man.

ARTEMISIA: It's her spiritual sense telling her to kill herself.

HILDEGARD: No, it isn't! Her spiritual sense would tell her that she was untouched by physical violation.

ARTEMISIA: *Untouched* by rape?

HILDEGARD: She does not have to identify with her body's experience.

ARTEMISIA: *(Exasperated.)* What are you talking about? That's exactly *why* she was able to murder herself!

HILDEGARD: *(Very calm.)*She took her physical life because she was not in touch with her spiritual one.

ARTEMISIA: *(Enraged.)* She killed herself, because she wasn't allowed to kill the rapist!

HILDEGARD: *(Turning to the audience.)* Well, you certainly do have an affinity for violent themes.

ARTEMISIA: *(Crossing down left, very angry.)* I knew it. Is this the lecture where you tell me how unladylike my subjects are? How a "woman artist" shouldn't paint naked women or acts of violence, because these are what men like to paint?

HILDEGARD: It's no concern of mine what you do or don't paint.

ARTEMISIA: Oh, really? But isn't that what makes "women artists" so special?

HILDEGARD: Women artists do have a different aesthetic.

ARTEMISIA: And that aesthetic includes fruit bowls and landscapes, doesn't it?—with maybe the occasional madonna and child. But it doesn't include dead men, does it?—or women with sharp objects!

HILDEGARD: I think you're putting words in my mouth. I don't see where I've criticized any of your paintings here today.

ARTEMISIA: *(Crossing down right.)* No. You've just ignored them. That's what women always do. They'll "ooh" and "aah" over the latest male discovery, but when it comes to my work, they get very quiet and pass on to the next painting. Unless, of course, they think I'm a man. Then I get judged by an entirely different standard.

HILDEGARD: *(Shaking her head.)* It sounds like you've had some very unfortunate experiences with women.

ARTEMISIA: Very.

HILDEGARD: That's really too bad, because women can be tremendously supportive and nurturing.

ARTEMISIA: I've never seen it.

HILDEGARD: Maybe you should come to Rupertsberg.

ARTEMISIA: *(Crossing down left with a laugh.)* That's the last place I should go!

HILDEGARD: What makes you say that?

ARTEMISIA: *(Exploding.)*
Because in Rupertsberg, you haven't got any critical standards! How can you when every woman is apparently inspired by God! I can just see it—First I would be told how limited representational art is—how "left brain!" I would have to hear this from women whose draftsmanship is so rotten they have to make a virtue out of inaccuracy. And then I would have to hear how"technique" is just a male substitute for inspiration, and what I really need to focus on is my emotional blocks. Then I would get the lecture on the morally corrosive effects of depicting sex and violence. This from women whose art is insipid and totally unoriginal, *but* toeing the party line. And then I would hear how compulsive I am about my work, from women who don't have the discipline to take themselves seriously. And finally—and here we're getting to the heart of the matter—I would be patronized by a pack of sanctimonious losers for the crass commercialism of actually trying to make a living off my art—when they'd be lucky if they could *give* their work away!

HILDEGARD: *(Deathly calm, speaking to the audience.)* You know, I didn't think it would be a good idea to have a panel without a moderator, and I think it's especially awkward when one of the artists on the panel openly hates women and personally attacks the other speaker.

ARTEMISIA: What are you talking about? You've been attacking me from the minute you set foot on this stage! You and your shit about"women artists!" What a hypocrite! You want to talk survival strategies? How about "Watch out for other women?'

HILDEGARD: Well, I don't need to.

ARTEMISIA: Yes, you do.

HILDEGARD: Since you don't seem to believe me, I suggest you come to Rupertsberg and see for yourself.

ARTEMISIA: On one condition.

HILDEGARD: What's that?

ARTEMISIA: You have to tell the truth.

HILDEGARD: What do you mean?

ARTEMISIA: I mean tell them that you taught yourself how to read and write—that it was candles after curfew, not some bolt of lightning from the blue, that lit up your consciousness! Tell them that it was you, not the Holy Spirit, who dictated your manuscripts! Tell them that the visions you have are a product of your own imagination, not transmissions from the spirit world, and that your mystical comas were nothing but sit-down strikes! Tell them that you make your art to please yourself, not God, and that you are an abbess with an international reputation, not through divine grace, but because you happen to be one hell of a diplomat, a very clever politician, a woman of enormous ambition who enjoys being on top—and who will do anything to stay there! You tell your little sisters of charity that you *earned* your power over them, and that the way you earned it was by being better than all of them! *(Quietly.)* Tell them that, and then let's see how supportive your community is.

HILDEGARD: *(Nodding her head at an old story.)* Well, Artemisia, I think we're back where we started from, aren't we? *(To the audience.)* Didn't I say this would happen? *(She sighs.)* You see, men—and women who think like them—cannot possibly comprehend the phenomenon of women's spirituality. All they can do is try to explain it away in terms of something they do understand. And that something, as Artemisia has so *masterfully* demonstrated, is self-interest.*(Patronizingly, to ARTEMISIA.)* I am afraid your attack on me is only an indictment of yourself.

ARTEMISIA: *(Disgusted, she sits.)* Why don't you tell the truth?

HILDEGARD: *(Considering her for a moment.)*You know, Artemisia, you're right. I'm not being honest. It's not honest of me to sit here and put up with your abuse. *(She rises and crosses in*

150

*front of the podium.)* It's not fair to me, it's not fair to my art, and it's not fair to these women who came here tonight expecting to hear something which would empower them. I wish there had been some representative from the theatre [university, etc.] here, but since there isn't, I'm going to have to take responsibility for the situation myself. I am going to ask the audience to pass a resolution tonight protesting your inclusion on this panel. *(Crossing down left.)* Furthermore, I am going to ask this audience to ban any woman who represents the male art establishment from participation in women's art events, whether they are gallery shows, panels, or conferences. The presence of these gender traitors is disruptive and divisive, derailing women's agendas and sidetracking our issues. Women like you, Artemisia, belong with the male institutions which have fostered you. You would be happier there, and we would certainly be happier too. The men love women like you. They would have loved everything you said tonight. You are just the kind of woman-hating woman they are always looking to hire for their token positions. You should stick with the men, Artemisia. And we should have the right to demand that you leave the stage, and that is exactly the resolution I am calling for now.

ARTEMISIA: *(Rising abruptly.)*Never mind. You don't have to take a vote. *(She begins to collect her notes.)*I should have known this would happen as soon as I put my work up on the screen. It's just too good, isn't it? Too good to have been done by a woman. You notice all this talk has been about my politics or my personality. You notice none of it has been about the art. But then, that's just like a man, isn't it, to want to focus on the actual work?

HILDEGARD: We *are* talking about the art. We are talking about the art that you are using like a weapon against other women.

*(ARTEMISIA has been getting her notes together during HILDEGARD's speech. As she starts to leave the podium, she accidentally drops her notes. She is kneeling on the floor collecting them during the remainder of HILDEGARD's speech. HILDEGARD reacts with a childlike petulance to ARTEMISIA's attempt to abandon her.)*

151

HILDEGARD: Most of us don't have the privilege of walking out on each other. Because for most of us, that would be walking out on ourselves. We have nowhere else to go. We don't have status as honorary men. Even when it gets too painful, we still have to stay and listen to each other. We have to work through our fears and our jealousies and our betrayals. *(ARTEMISIA starts to exit, and HILDEGARD pursues her.)* We can't go running back to the men, because for most of us, men are the enemy!

ARTEMISIA: *(Enraged, she turns to confront HILDEGARD, who, surprised by ARTEMISIA's vehemence, backs up. ARTEMISIA returns to the podium.)* And you think they aren't mine? You think I don't know what men are about? Look at my paintings! Bring up my last slide! *(The Florentine Judith Slaying Holofernes comes up.)*

HILDEGARD: *(Standing next to ARTEMISIA.)* I believe we've already seen this one.

ARTEMISIA: No, you haven't. This is my second version. I painted it ten years after I did the first one. Do you know why I did that? Look at it! It's two women cutting off the head of a man. Why do you think I painted the same picture twice? Because I like men? Because they've been so good to me?

HILDEGARD: *(Sitting in ARTEMISIA's chair.)* Because it sells.

ARTEMISIA: Because when I was sixteen, my art teacher, my precious *male* art teacher that you seem to think it was such a privilege to study under, came into my bedroom and raped me. And then my father, the famous painter Orazio Gentileschi—the one you think was such a great mentor to me—my own father made me go to court and testify about the rape, because he couldn't stand the fact that one of his colleagues had stolen his property. It didn't have anything to do with me. I was just a token in their artistic rivalry. And the judge had me tortured to see if I was telling the truth. He didn't torture the rapist, who lied through his teeth, telling everybody what a whore I was. And they had two midwives—two *women*—put their hands in my vagina to inspect me—right there in front of a clerk! Do you think my father cared about me at all when he let them do that? And where were the women? Well, my mother had died when I was twelve. And then there was my best friend, Tuzia, who lived upstairs from me. Do you know who it was who arranged to let the rapist into the house when my father wasn't home? Tuzia. She was in on it with him. Why? Because I can paint! Because I wasn't going to have to fuck for a living, legally or not, and she couldn't stand the idea. And neither can you! Neither can any woman! *(HILDEGARD starts to say something in her defense, but ARTEMISIA cuts her off.)* But I didn't kill myself like Lucretia, because I was that good. A friend of the family was "kind" enough to rescue my reputation by marrying me, and then the Medicis were "generous" enough to give me commissions after the trial. But don't think that I didn't know that my damaged goods made great bargains for my rescuers. Rescuers and rapists are in the same business. Yes, I got rid of the husband, but I still have to make a living. And don't think that just because I get professional commissions that they're ever as high as male painters get. Or on time. Or paid in full. It doesn't matter how long I've been painting, or how good I am, because I'm always a woman, and that means I'm always an amateur. And you want to give me shit, because I don't walk around advertising the fact I'm a "woman artist!"

HILDEGARD: *(Patronizing ARTEMISIA.)* You should have told us about the rape earlier.

ARTEMISIA: Why? So you could patronize me, like you're doing now? Does the fact I've been sexually violated and publicly humiliated suddenly make it okay for me to paint so well? Am I neutralized enough for you? Does it mean my dues are all paid up in the Women's Club? Just because you think sadism was good for your soul, doesn't mean you get to inflict your pain on me!

HILDEGARD: *(Shocked and confused.)* What do you mean, "sadism?"

ARTEMISIA: What your family did to you.

HILDEGARD: *(Confused.)* My family?

ARTEMISIA: *(Exasperated.)* Your family! For chrissake, they locked you up in a cell for ten years, because they wanted to get rid of you!

HILDEGARD: It was the will of God...

ARTEMISIA: Ten children and the youngest one sick all the time—probably an invalid for life. Pretty convenient, this will of God.

HILDEGARD: That is not true! I was more loved than any of my brothers and sisters!

ARTEMISIA: Oh, give me a break! Parents who love their children don't send them to prison.

HILDEGARD: It was a monastery, not a prison!

ARTEMISIA: What the hell is the difference to an eight-year old? You never saw the sun, you never felt the rain, you never rolled on the grass, you never had any playmates—

HILDEGARD: *(Cutting her off.)* I have been amply compensated by the gifts of the spirit!

ARTEMISIA: *(Pausing to consider HILDEGARD.)* You are one hell of survivor. I've got to hand it to you, Hildegard. I don't know how anyone could turn ten years of torture into some kind of privilege, but you managed to do it. Somehow your little eight-year old brain flipped the whole thing around, so that not only weren't you abandoned by your parents, but you were somehow more loved than the rest of the family—more loved in fact than any other child in the history of the world! And I have no doubt that this fiction kept you alive all those years, but somebody inside there knows the real truth. And that somebody must be pissed as hell. No wonder you've got headaches all the time.

HILDEGARD: You don't understand God's love.

ARTEMISIA: That may be true, but I'll tell you this—If anyone ever tried to take my daughter away, I'd kill them with my bare hands.

HILDEGARD: The male-identified woman can only meet violence with violence.

ARTEMISIA: The male-identified woman is *you*, Hildegard! The male-identified woman meets violence with denial!

HILDEGARD: Instead of using your rape as an opportunity for spiritual growth, you have let your hatred and anger turn inward and fester—allowing it to corrupt your art—

ARTEMISIA: *(Exploding with rage.)* You are so full of shit!

HILDEGARD: *(Rising and crossing to ARTEMISIA.)* I am not your enemy, Artemisia. I am trying to be supportive.

ARTEMISIA: The hell you are! You're trying to convert me. You're trying to convert all of us! You want to ask these women to get rid of me? All right, fine! But first let's ask them what they think about you! *(She addresses the audience.)* How many of you think Hildegard von Bingen was abused as a child? Come on—Raise your hands! How many of you think she was abused? *(Assuming there is a show of hands at this point.)* How many of you think her parents didn't love her? Come on! Let's see it! *(Assuming another show of hands.)* And how many of you think locking an eight-year old in a cell was an atrocity? *(Another show of hands.)*

HILDEGARD: *(Struggling to maintain control.)* Well... Congratulations, Artemisia. It appears you have won the debate.

ARTEMISIA: I wasn't competing.

HILDEGARD: Even better! To win when it looks like you weren't even trying! *(ARTEMISIA gives up. She turns to go.)* Aren't you going to stay and savor your victory?

ARTEMISIA: What's the point?

HILDEGARD: The point is, you get to stay and tell us more about the secret art of killing men. *(She gestures toward the painting.)*

ARTEMISIA: There's no secret, Hildegard. It takes two women to do it.

*(ARTEMISIA exits. HILDEGARD turns to look at the painting. The lights come down slowly, pausing to linger on the images of Judith and Abra.)*

**BLACKOUT**

**END OF PLAY**

# ACKNOWLEDGEMENTS

First, I would like to thank all of the women, and the men, who have booked my own performances of *The Second Coming of Joan of Arc*. I have toured in the piece for twenty years, and I have so many wonderful memories from the communities I visited and the folks who produced me and hosted me. Some of these producers had to face down the disapproval of their colleagues, defend their right to produce women-only performances, and be very creative about raising money for the shows.

A special thanks to Mary Bryne and the National Women's Music Festival, to Lee Glanton of Campfest, to Lisa Vogl of the Michigan Womyn's Music Festival, and to Trish Williams, who introduced me to the wonderful community of lesbians in Florida. And thank you, Sarah Valentine, for encouraging me to come out of early retirement from performing as Joan!

I also want to express my appreciation to the women who have performed my work, and especially the solo shows. Debra Wright has performed more of my plays than any actor, and it has been my privilege to direct her as Calamity Jane, Artemisia Gentileschi, and Charlotte Cushman. She has been an inspiration to me as a writer, as well as a friend.

I also want to thank Irene Reti, founder of Herbooks, who published *The Second Coming of Joan of Arc* in the first collection of my plays. Even after she closed the press, she generously continued to distribute the book, in order to keep it in print.

I am grateful to Sara Yager, the designer of the cover, who has been so generous with her artwork.

**ORIGINALLY PUBLISHED:**

*The Second Coming of Joan of Arc* was originally published in *Sinister Wisdom,* Vol. 35 (Summer/Fall 1988) Berkeley, CA

*The Last Reading of Charlotte Cushman* was originally published in *Voices Made Flesh: Performing Women's Autobiography*, edited by Lynn C. Miller, Jacqueline Taylor, and M. Heather Carver, University of Wisconsin Press, Madison, 2003.

*The Parmachene Belle* was originally published in *The Harrington Lesbian Fiction Quarterly,* Vol. 4, No. 1, 2003, Binghamton, NY.

*'Cookin' with Typhoid Mary* and *Calamity Jane Sends a Message to Her Daughter* were originally published in *The Second Coming of Joan of Arc and Other Plays* by Carolyn Gage, Herbooks, Inc. Santa Cruz, CA, 1994.

*Harriet Tubman Visits a Therapist* was originally published in *Off-Off Broadway Festival Plays, Twenty-Third Series*, Samuel French, Inc., NYC.

# OTHER BOOKS BY CAROLYN GAGE

*Nine Short Plays*
*Black Eye and Other Short Plays*
*Three Comedies*
*The Triple Goddess: Three Plays*
*The Spindle and Other Lesbian Fairy Tales*
*Starting from Zero: One-Act Plays about Lesbians in Love*
*Monologues and Scenes for Lesbian Actors*
*Take Stage! How to Direct and Produce a Lesbian Play*
*Sermons for a Lesbian Tent Revival*
*Supplemental Sermons for a Lesbian Tent Revival*
*Hotter Than Hell: The 2011 Lesbian Tent Revival*
*Like There's No Tomorrow: Meditations for Women Leaving Patriarchy*
*The Gaia Papers: A Search for a Science of Gaia*
*13 Propositions for Rewiring the Lesbian Brain*

CPSIA information can be obtained
at www.ICGtesting.com
Printed in the USA
LVHW030309310821
696470LV00004B/744

9 781105 941672